# LIVES

OF THE

# CHIEF FATHERS OF NEW ENGLAND.

The Lord our God be with us, as he was with our fathers: let him not leave us, nor forsake us.

1 Kings 8 ; 57.

## VOL. VI.

# THE LIFE

OF

# THOMAS HOOKER.

BY EDWARD W. HOOKER.

LIBRARY EDITION, 100 COPIES.

BOSTON:
1870.

# PREFACE.

THE preparation of this volume of the Series has been delayed, beyond the expectations of the author and of the Committee of Publication. This delay has arisen from the pressure of other duties, and from the difficulty of collecting materials. The latter has been of no ordinary magnitude. In the almost total absence of original papers of any kind, from Mr. Hooker's pen, the author has been compelled to rely principally upon matter, relative to him, which was incidental in Puritan and New England history, and scattered through many volumes in various libraries, and upon many thousands of pages. The reader will find in this volume, therefore, little of autobiography. The history of Mr. Hooker's life in Connecticut, especially, has been found merged in the civil and religious history of the State. The scantiness of original materials has been rendered a matter for special regret, from the belief that there have been in existence rich materials for a far more full biography, had they been carefully preserved. At the taking down of the old parsonage house of the First Congregational Church in Hartford, about thirty years since, a large quantity of ancient papers was found, supposed to be those of Rev. Thomas Hooker; and by persons employed in the work, and who were either ignorant or thoughtless of their value, they were thrown into Connecticut river. If any thing would justify a State enactment, making the careless or wanton destruction of ancient manuscript papers felony, and punishable as such, the occurrence of such cases as this,—which are frequent,—would seem to do so. If, like many good and great men, Thomas Hooker was accustomed to record, in a journal form or otherwise, interesting incidents in his own life, his religious exercises, and results of his experience and observation as a Christian citizen and a minister, such records have been hopelessly put beyond the reach of any biographer.

With its many imperfections, from whatever cause, the present volume is commended to the lovers of the Puritan character and principles, in hope that it will be found not altogether without value, as a small contribution to the stock of Christian biography. E. W. H.

*May*, 1849.

# LIFE OF THOMAS HOOKER.

## CHAPTER I.

Parentage and ancestry. Cotemporaries. Persecutions of the Puritans of his time. Education at Cambridge. Fellowship in Emmanuel College. Conversion, religious experience, and formation of character. Preaches at Chelmsford. Remarkable success and influence. Character of his eloquence as a preacher.

THE eminence and usefulness of a great and good man invariably lead us to inquire into his early history; his parentage, ancestry, and early education; and the providential circumstances which gave direction to his mind, and stamp to his character. We generally have the means of answering such inquiries; are permitted to see what the individual was in his childhood, youth, and advancing manhood; how his character was formed, and by what instrumentalities developed. And while we see how men have been rendered useful, influential and estimable, we are instructed respecting the methods by which we are to labor for the formation of character in those whom we are to educate for the service of God and the good of the world.

There are cases, however, in which Divine Providence denies us the satisfaction of this description of knowledge. The early history of the individual is hidden from our view. No friend or admirer of his character has preserved the materials for his early biography; or if so, they remain as yet undiscovered, if not lost. We have therefore to begin with the man after he has grown up to his full intellectual and moral stature. We doubt not he had an early education, and a course of training for his sphere of effort and usefulness. But we have to repress our curiosity on these points, and to rest satisfied that such a man lives and is become a blessing to the world; and be willing to leave the unknown years of his early life to be shown as among the secret things to be revealed in eternity.

The case of the excellent Thomas Hooker was like that which has now been described. Nothing has come down to us, in the histories of him and of his times, which even answers the question who were his father and mother. His birthplace was Marfield, Leicestershire,

England. His birthday was July 7, 1586. All which is known of him from that day till his entrance upon his collegiate course, is comprised in two sentences of the biographical sketch given by the author of Magnalia Americana. "He was born of parents that were neither unable nor unwilling to bestow upon him a liberal education : whereunto the early lively sparkles of wit observed in him did very much encourage them. His natural temper was cheerful and courteous ; but it was accompanied with such a sensible grandeur of mind, as caused his friends, without the help of astrology, to prognosticate that he was born to be considerable."

We commence our history of him, then, as a student in Emmanuel college, Cambridge ; with his character mainly formed, and his preparations made for the life he was to lead and for the work he was to do, as a man, a christian, and a minister of Christ.

It would be matter of curiosity rather than of importance to investigate the ancestry of Thomas Hooker, and to follow out the ramifications of lineage which would show the collateral relationships of his family. Perhaps we should find him related to Richard Hooker, the great apologist for English Episcopacy, and styled by king James, " the judicious." The existence of any relationship of consanguinity between these two men, however, is more than we have been able to discover. It is of very little consequence, moreover, in this sketch.

If, however, there was such relationship, it is a matter of interest to the student of coincidences and contrasts, that these two men, of the same family name, and living in England cotemporaries for several years, should have thought, reasoned, and written so utterly at variance with each other on the great subject of Ecclesiastical Polity: Richard Hooker having written his great work which has given such strength and permanence to both English and American Episcopacy; and Thomas Hooker, on the other hand, having been the author of another system of Church Polity, of an entirely different character from that of his illustrious namesake; and appearing as a master-builder among the churches of New England, upon the broad and scriptural foundation of a most decided and energetic Congregationalism; and this not only as distinguished from Episcopacy, but even from Presbyterianism. There were strong points of resemblance between the two men, in the essential elements of their characters, both as men and as christians. At the same time they were diametrically opposite in their Ecclesiastical views. We are thus shown that it is quite possible for two men, of the same nation, language, name, and perhaps lineage,—both Protestants, and of essentially the same religious belief,—to think, write and teach in wide difference from each other on matters ecclesiastical, and to lay the foundations of two separate Protestant religious denominations, never brought into union, and generally living in controversy with each other; and yet neither of these two men be found "grievously possessed with a devil," nor deserving to be shut out of the other's charity as a christian. If in generations past, it has run in the blood of the Hookers to construct systems of ecclesiastical government, it is very clear that,—blood notwithstanding,—one may be an inflexible Churchman, and the other an equally inflexible Congregationalist; and that, while the same kind of blood may run in their veins, and in the same directions, their processes of thinking on such a subject as ecclesiastical polity may run in stubborn and absolute opposition to each other, and the results of their investigations and reasonings be as wide asunder as the east is from the west. Placed side by side, the two men form a study, for the moral painter, of no ordinary interest. The things to respect, admire and love, in each, are many. Widely as they differed in their views of the government of the church, imperfect and agitated with divisions and conflicts on earth, they still had so many points of harmony on the great articles of the New Testament faith, and so many resemblances, in their spirit, to that of the gospel of Jesus Christ, that we will hope they have, together, seen ages of love, harmony and bliss, as members of the Church perfect, peaceful, and glorified in heaven.

Thomas Hooker, as the cotemporary of Cotton, Shepard, Norton, and others of their spirit, lived in England at a period when good men were sorely tried with wickedness in the high places of the Church as well as of the State. He lived in the time of king James I., and of Archbishop Laud ; and also of the Council Table, the Star Chamber, and the Court of High Commission,—three tribunals, of which Puritans lived day and night in fear. No man who loved his Bible and the religious liberty it teaches, was at any time sure, that by some mandate emanating from men in the interest of the ecclesiastical establishment, he should not on some pretext or other, be summoned before one of these courts, or before his bishop ; and pass thence to Bridewell, or the Limbo; to Newgate, the Fleet, or the Compters; to the Clink, the Gate House, or the White Lion—for imprisonment during the pleasure of his persecutors, and probably for life.

Thus much, only, it is necessary to say in the present volume, of the "troublous times" in which Hooker lived, that we may estimate aright the circumstances in which his christian and ministerial character was formed. And with this reference to the history of a period already before our readers in former volumes of this Series of Lives, we shall confine this narrative principally to Hooker's personal history and character, apart from any farther views of the times in which he lived in England.

While most men who enter the christian ministry, under the influence of divine grace, are found fitted for its duties generally considered, some appear to have been designed and prepared, by Divine Providence, for peculiar and difficult departments of the ministerial work, and in which lies their great strength and their special usefulness. One is particularly qualified to be a defender of the great articles of the christian faith; another to be a learned and critical expositor of the word of God; a third to be a faithful and energetic promoter of the revival of religion and of the purification of the churches. One is a "son of thunder," and another "a son of consolation." Each of these "has his proper gift of God; one after this manner and another after that." Each fulfills a peculiar mission, as having a special relation to the kingdom of God, to be advanced in the hearts of believers. Mr. Hooker was one of those ministers who appear to have been designed for a particular service in the church. It was one which he faithfully and successfully fulfilled, both to christians of his time, by his preaching and personal counsels; and to the generations of the church following, by his published works. The manner of his conversion, and the course of exercises through which he was carried by the Divine Spirit, before he became fully established in the enjoyment of the divine consolations, fitted him for the particular work of a "son of consolation." It is the more worthy of notice in his case, as his were times when "the prince of this world" employed himself with unwonted and malignant diligence to "wear out the saints of the Most High," by stirring up against all serious christians, not conforming to the rites and ceremonies of the established church, the spirit of ecclesiastical oppression and persecution. And those who have had most trying experience of this policy of the adversary, have had occasion to know, that when "the devil is come down having great wrath, knowing that he hath but a short time," his "fiery darts" are many, and the spiritual sufferings of the people of God through them are often deep and distressing.

It appears that Mr. Hooker's conversion took place while he was a Fellow of Emmanuel college; and that his mind, after having been matured by thorough educational discipline, was rendered the seat of spiritual sufferings which prostrated the scholar and the man of intellectual might, low at the foot of "the cross.' The history of this eventful period of his life, is thus given, by one who had studied the ways in which God leads those whom he has appointed to important services.

"It pleased the Spirit of God very powerfully to break into the soul of this person, with such a sense of his being exposed unto the just wrath of heaven, as filled him with most unusual degrees of horror and anguish, which broke not only his rest, but his heart also; and caused him to cry out, 'While I suffer thy terrors, O Lord, I am distracted.' While he long had a soul harrassed with such distresses, he had a singular help in the prudent and piteous carriage of

Mr. Ash, who was a sizer that then waited on him, and attended him with such discreet and proper compassion as made him afterwards to respect him highly, all his days. He afterwards gave this account of himself: 'That in the time of his agonies he could reason himself to the rule, and conclude that there was no way but submission to God and lying at the foot of his mercy in Christ Jesus, and waiting humbly there till he should please to persuade the soul of his favor; nevertheless, when he came to apply this rule unto himself in his own condition, his reason would fail him, and he was able to do nothing.'"

Let it not be said this was intellectual weakness, yielding to melancholic or enthusiastic feelings. Here was "the strong man," bowing under a pressure which he could not sustain; the man of intellectual might, conscious in his inmost soul that he could not withstand "the Spirit of the Lord God," convincing him of his sinfulness both natural and practical; of his spiritual peril, as exposed to the penalties of the divine law, which is "holy, and just, and good." The awakened and convicted hearers of Peter on the day of Pentecost, the prostrated "Saul of Tarsus," and the trembling jailer of

* Mather's Magnalia, I., 303.

Philippi, all had felt thus. In these spiritual exercises, Mr. Hooker experienced those distresses of the soul which always in a greater or less degree precede true conversion and a saving reconciliation with God.

"Having been a considerable time thus troubled with such impressions of 'the spirit of bondage' as were to fit him for the great services and enjoyments which God designed for him, at length he received "the spirit of adoption," with well-grounded persuasion of his interest in the new covenant."*

The transition from these deep distresses of soul to the "strong consolation" which is in Christ Jesus, must have made "the new man" to appear in very striking contrast with himself as he was in the days of his sorrows. This man, once so miserable, was so sweetly brought into the light and comfort of the gospel, that a record like the following could be made respecting him: "It became his manner at his lying down for sleep, in the evening, to single out some certain promise of God, which he would repeat and ponder, and keep his heart close unto it; until he found that satisfaction of soul with which he could say, 'I will both lay me

* Magnalia, I. 303.

down in peace and sleep; for thou, Lord, only, makest me dwell in safety.' And he would afterwards counsel others to take the same course; telling them, 'that the promise was the boat which was to carry a perishing sinner over unto the Lord Jesus Christ.'"*

A point of great practical importance to christians of a desponding habit, is here presented, and to which particular attention should be called. The tendency in some children of God, to look upon the dark and gloomy side of their own case, and to lay to heart in a discouraging way every rebuke of conscience and of precept, while at the same time they dare not take to themselves the consolations of a divine promise, needs, as we think, to be corrected, by fixing the mind upon some of the "exceeding great and precious promises" of the gospel. A determinate act of the christian for this very purpose is many times needful. He must not wait till an almost miraculous enforcement of some divine promise is made upon his attention, while he is brooding over his sins and nourishing his sorrows, as though here were all the duties he had to do. Let him resolve, "I will seek unto God, and unto God will I commit my

* Magnalia, I. 303.

cause." Let him do this, in looking into his good word, for something which shall show him a ground of hope, and open some spring of consolation. Let him think upon it and lay it to his heart, as having as much right there, as any precept of the gospel; and let him be thankful for the certainty that God as much delights in that filial faith, which with a firm hand grasps his promises, as he does in that obedience which conforms to his precepts. Let such a christian continually remember that scripture, "Thus saith the High and Lofty One that inhabiteth eternity, whose name is Holy: I dwell in the high and holy place, with him also that is of a contrite and humble spirit, to revive the spirit of the humble, and to revive the heart of the contrite ones." That believer, slain by the law and broken in spirit for his sins, who, like Thomas Hooker, will habitually lie down at night meditating upon the promises of a faithful God and a mighty Saviour, will be able to rise each morning, saying, "And my sleep was sweet unto me;" he will go on with a strength, alacrity and cheerfulness in the performance of the daily duties of the christian life, to which despondency and feeble faith would otherwise keep him very much a stranger.

This part of Mr. Hooker's training for the

ministry was of an importance to him in his after life, not surpassed by all his attainments in human learning and theological science. It strengthened the intellectually strong man, and made him to be, like Bunyan's Great-Heart, an invaluable guide to Zion's pilgrims, and a valiant defender of the feeble and trembling believers, against the "accuser of the brethren."

When a minister "neglects not such a gift that is in him," but cultivates it, and keeps it bright and ready for use, God will give him opportunities to use it. Mr. Hooker in the earliest years of his work as a minister and guide to souls, found much of this kind of work to perform. "At his first leaving of the university, he sojourned in the house of Mr. Drake, a gentleman of great note, not far from London, whose worthy consort being visited with such distresses of soul as Mr. Hooker himself had passed through, it proved an unspeakable advantage to both of them that he had an opportunity of being serviceable; for indeed he had now no superior, and scarce any equal, for the skill of treating a troubled soul. When he left Mr. Drake's family, he did more publicly and frequently preach about London; and in a little time he became famous for his ministerial abilities, but especially for his notable faculty at the wise and fit management of wounded spirits." * Precious privilege of the sympathizing minister of Christ! to be his Master's agent in imparting to "them that mourn in Zion," "the oil of joy for mourning, and the garments of praise for the spirit of heaviness."

But there was still another qualification for the christian ministry, kindred to this, which Mr. Hooker possessed in an eminent degree, and which has been thus described: "He had a singular ability at giving answers to cases of conscience; whereof happy was the experience of some thousands. For this work he usually set apart the second day of the week, wherein he admitted all sorts of persons, in their discourses with him to receive the benefit of the extraordinary experience which himself had found of Satan's devices. Once, particularly, Mr. Hooker was addressed by a student in divinity, who, entering upon his ministry, was horridly buffeted with temptations, which were become almost intolerable. Repairing to Mr. Hooker, in the distresses and anguish of his mind, and bemoaning his own overwhelming fears, while the lion was thus roaring at him, Mr. Hooker answered, 'I can compare with any

* Magnalia, I. 304.

man living, for fears. My advice to you is, that you search out and analyze the humbling causes for them, and refer them to their proper places; then go and pour them out before the Lord; and they shall prove more profitable than any book you can read.'" *

But Mr. Hooker in his dealing with troubled consciences, observed that there were a sort of crafty and guileful souls, (which he would find out with admirable dexterity,) and of these he would say, as Paul of the Cretians, "Wherefore rebuke them sharply, that they may be sound in the faith." Sharp rebukes make sound christians. Of some, indeed, he "had compassion, making a difference," and others he "saved with fear pulling them out of the fire." †

This was a point of skill which could have come of no ordinary measure of christian experience, nor of a limited acquaintance with christian people in the circumstances of spiritual perplexity which often arise under temptations from without or from within. To guide such souls aright, according to the sure word of God, and also safely, for their establishment and peace, is among the most difficult and critical of the duties of the ministry. In reference to his

* Magnalia, I. 304. † Ibid.

preparation for such work, the minister needs to remember the words of his Master, " This kind goeth not out but by prayer and fasting."

Mr. Hugh Peters, in a history of his christian experience, addressed to his daughters, shortly before his death, attested the comfort he derived from " the love and labors of Mr. Thomas Hooker."

And yet, this minister, who was so eminently " a son of consolation" to the afflicted children of God, was a perfect " son of thunder," when he had occasion to rebuke sin. The remark has been quaintly made of him, that " while doing his Master's work, he would put a king in his pocket." The moral courage thus attributed to him was illustrated on the occasion of a national fast, when the duty devolved upon him of preaching at Chelmsford, before the judges, then on their circuit. Their presence and that of a vast congregation, did not prevent his " declaring freely the sins of England and the plagues that would come for such sins." And in his prayer he besought the God of heaven to set on the heart of the king what his own mouth had spoken in the 2d chapter of Malachi, 11th and 12th verses, quoting them in his prayer, distinctly, as follows : " An abomination is committed ; Judah hath married the daughter of a strange god ; the Lord will cut off the man that doeth this." It would seem that the consciences of the judges in whose presence he thus fearlessly preached and solemnly prayed, were on his side ; for they took no other notice of what he did, than to turn to the passages he had so quoted and applied.

That his fidelity in reproof at this time was remembered against him at a subsequent period, when he was under the displeasure of the ecclesiastical authorities, is highly probable. Certain it is, however, that if fearlessness of speech could afford a pretext for his being called to account by the enemies of truth and godliness, it did so ; for he took no care to repress the impulses which he felt to the performance of his duty. And that which he did in the presence of judges of the king's bench, he would doubtless have done in the presence of "the king's most excellent majesty" himself.

Mr. Hooker's education was such an one as the ancient and honorable university of Cambridge could give. The fact that he held a fellowship in his college, and was for a time in its board of instruction, affords presumptive evidence that his intellectual powers and his attainments in learning were held in high esteem, in the university. Added to this, it appears that he preached the gospel, to good acceptance, within the literary atmosphere of Cambridge; where no ordinary man could have sustained himself as a preacher.

Additional to his labors as an instructor and a preacher, his influence was of value to the university, in promoting the reformation of some existing abuses. He was in his appropriate sphere, moreover, to exert an important influence upon the christian ministry; Emmanuel college being the residence of those who were designed for the sacred office. After leaving Cambridge, he for some time preached occasionally at London.*

His unimposing entrance upon the ministry, has been thus described, "He was not ambitious to exercise his ministry among the great ones of the world, from whom preferment might be expected; but in this imitating the example and character of our blessed Saviour, of whom it is noted, according to the prophecy of Isaiah by him, 'The poor have the gospel preached unto them;' he chose to be where great numbers of the poor could receive the gospel from him."†

The field of Mr. Hooker's principal labors as

* Mag. I, 304.

† Holmes' Hist. Camb., p. 39.

a preacher, while residing in England, was Chelmsford, in Essex. His own strong inclinations were to reside in Colchester; that he might be near the Rev. Mr. Rogers of Dedham, and attend upon his lectures. For Mr. Rogers as a preacher, he seems to have had a very high esteem, and he called him the prince of all the preachers of England. The great Lord and Master of ministers, however, had other designs respecting Mr. Hooker. He himself felt that it was "not in man that walketh to direct his steps," and once said "that the providence of God often diverted him from employment in such places as he himself desired, and still directed him to such places as he had no thoughts of." The particular object for which he was invited to exercise his ministry in Chelmsford, was that he might be a lecturer, and an assistant of the Rev. Mr. Mitchell. In this intimacy and association with the minister of Chelmsford, was illustrated that excellency in the general character of Mr. Hooker, that he was of a truly fraternal spirit: living and laboring in that harmony of views and feelings with his brethren, which rendered both his and their labors happy, and testified to other men of the times, the excellent spirit of the Puritan ministry.

Mr. Hooker's ministry at Chelmsford was

continued for the period of four years. He enjoyed a popularity,—in the best sense of the term,—unsurpassed by that of any minister of his day. The attendance on his preaching was large. Among his hearers were noblemen, and others of high standing in English society. The influence of his ministry was powerfully and extensively felt throughout that country. The characteristics and impressions of his preaching have been thus stated by the author of Magnalia Americana: "There was a rare mixture of pleasure and profit in his preaching. His hearers felt those penetrating impressions of his ministry upon their souls which caused them to reverence him as 'a teacher sent from God.' He had a most excellent faculty at the application of his doctrine. He would therein so touch the consciences of his auditors, that a judicious person would say of him that he was the best at an use that he ever heard.* Hereby there was a great reformation wrought, not only in the town but in the adjacent country: from all parts whereof they came to hear the wisdom of the Lord Jesus Christ in his gospel, by this worthy man dispensed. When he first set up

* An allusion to the fashion of the Puritan preachers of that period of concluding their sermons with various uses of exhortations, &c. &c.

his lectures there was more profaneness than devotion in the town. The multitude of inns and shops in the town, produced one particular disorder, of people's filling the streets with unsuitable behavior, after the public services of the Lord's day were over. But the power of his ministry in public, and by the prudence of his carriage in private, he quickly cleared the streets of this disorder; and the Sabbath came to be very visibly sanctified among the people."*

For the secret of success so remarkable, and of influence so powerful, upon a community so far from godliness, we must look into the study and the closet of this great and good man. His diligent studies, sanctified by prayer, and his prayers procuring the gift of the Holy Spirit to attend his labors, were doubtless the causes, unseen and unsuspected by the thoughtless world around him, of the public reformation.

Several incidents related of him and of some of his hearers, which occurred in the course of his ministry at Chelmsford and elsewhere in England, are worthy of note. They attest not only the talents and the influence of the man himself, but the presence and blessing of the Holy Spirit; and they illustrate that scripture,

---

* Magnalia, I. 304.

"Not by might, nor by power, but by my Spirit, saith the Lord."

"A profane person designing therein only an ungodly diversion and merriment, said to his companions, 'Come, let us go hear what that bawling Hooker will say to us:' and thereupon, with an intention to make sport, unto Chelmsford lecture they came. The man had not been long in the church, before the 'quick and powful word of God,' in the mouth of his faithful Hooker, pierced the soul of him. He came out with an awakened and distressed soul. By the farther blessing of God upon Mr. Hooker's ministry, he arrived unto a true conversion. For which cause he would not afterward leave that blessed ministry, but went a thousand leagues to attend it and enjoy it."*

"It was Mr. Hooker's manner; once a year to visit his native county. In one of those vis its he had an invitation to preach in the grea church of Leicester. One of the chief burgess es in the town much opposed his preaching there. And when he could not prevail to hinder it, he set certain fiddlers at work to disturb him, in the church porch, or church-yard. But such was the vivacity of Mr. Hooker, as to pro-

* Probably emigrated with, or followed him, to New England.

ceed in what he was about, without either the damping of his mind or the drowning of his voice; whereupon the man himself went to the church door, to overhear what he said. It pleased God so to accompany some words uttered by Mr. Hooker, as thereby to procure first the attention, and then the conviction of that wretched man. He then came to Mr. Hooker with a penitent confession of his wickedness; and became so penitent a convert, as to be, at length, a sincere professor and practicer of the godliness whereof he had been a persecutor."*

The accounts given of the preaching of Mr. Hooker justify the belief, that his eloquence was of a high order: not as having the oratorical finish which is obtained by men seeking fame and popularity with the multitude, but that eloquence which is produced by the pervading influence of truth upon the soul, and an earnest desire to bring that truth into immediate contact with the mind, the conscience, the sensibilities of the hearer. The description has been applied to him, and doubtless with justice, which has been given of Bucholtzer: "Vivida in eo omnia fuerunt; vivida vox; vivida occuli; vivida man-

* Mag. Book I, 307.

us; gestus omnes vivida."* One who seems to have studied his character and manner as a preacher, with the taste of both a christian and lover of sacred eloquence, says of him: "He not only had that which Quinctillian calls a natural movableness of soul, whereby the distinct images of things would come so nimbly and yet so fitly into his mind, that he could utter them with fluent expressions, as the old orators would usually ascribe unto a special assistance from heaven, and counted that men did therein speak divinely, but the rise of this fluency in him was the divine relish which he had of the things spoken: the sacred panting of his holy soul after the glorious objects of the invisible world; and the true zeal of religion giving fire to his discourses." "The vigor in the ministry of our Hooker, being raised by a coal from the altar of a most real devotion, touching his heart; it would be wrong unto the good Spirit of our God, if he should not be acknowledged the Author of it. The Spirit accordingly gave a wonderful and unusual success unto the ministry wherein he breathed so remarkably."†

Serious, experimental christians love to sit

* In him every thing was lively; a lively voice, lively eyes, lively hands, lively every gesture.

† Mag. Book III.

under such a ministry as now described; and in after life will often refer to it, as having been profitable to their spiritual interests. Thomas Shepard speaks with marked particularity, of the blessings he enjoyed at Chelmsford under the ministry of Mr. Weld and Mr. Hooker.*

It is delightful to see sacred eloquence thus traced to its true source. A blessed man is that minister, whose power over men's minds is thus derived. And blessed are the people who sit under such ministrations.

That such a preacher as Mr. Hooker should have been molested and hindered in his work by ecclesiastical authority, is to be accounted for by the fact that there ever have been those, who, instead of being satisfied with the power committed to them as instructors and shepherds to the flock of Christ, have made themselves "lords over God's heritage." Moreover the elevation of the standard of truth and holiness, in a faithful ministry is always offensive to those whose dependence is on "the form of godliness," while "denying the power thereof." Furthermore "the Prince of this world" has always shewed a particular spite against ministers whose instructions clearly discriminate, and assist in discerning

* Life of Shepard, p. 42.

"between him that serveth God and him that serveth him not;" and which set in clear light the distinctions between the false doctrines of men who love not the truth, and the doctrines of the uncorruptible word.

## CHAPTER II.

Mr. Hooker silenced from preaching; for what, and by whom. Effect upon his spirit and character. Review of his preparation for this trial. His influence at Chelmsford upon the Conformist ministers and others. His belief in the articles of the church. Bond for appearance before the Court of High Commission. Departure for Holland, and narrow escape from the pursuivants. Residence and ministry in Holland. Views of the religious state of Holland. Progress of the Puritan emigration from England to America; and objects of it. Returns from Holland to England, and great danger of arrest. Sails for New England. Farewell sermon. Effect of Hooker's and Cotton's removal, upon Shepard and others.

In the year 1630, a spiritual court which held its sessions in Chelmsford, the place of Mr. Hooker's residence, put an end to his preaching there. He had spent four years in the earnest endeavor to fulfill his ministry, in the "answer of a good conscience before God," at the same time declining conformity to what he deemed superstitious and useless externals, required of the ministry of the Established Church. He was not a man to be persuaded by rhetoric, or frightened by menace, or compelled by bonds and imprisonment, to encumber his ministrations in the word, ordinances, and prayer, with the paraphernalia of Popery, whether enjoined from the Vatican at Rome, or from the palace of "his grace the Archbishop of Canterbury." The simplicity of the gospel and of that form of service which regards God as "a Spirit" to be worshiped "in spirit and in truth," was not in his judgment to be marred by association with the display of surplices, caps, copes, cassocks, and other like matters of sanctimonious foppery, to which many attached so much importance. And more than this, he was one of the last men to feel any complacency in Popery whether under the garb of Protestant Episcopacy, or appearing as openly "The Beast." His influence also upon other ministers was exerted, without disguise or fear of consequences, to encourage and embolden them to take the position of unflinching resistance to all ecclesiastical impositions in matters which would directly or indirectly acknowledge the Romish religion.

Here, however, let it be observed, that Mr. Hooker was not a dissenter from "the doctrine of Faith of the Church of England." He simply wished for his brethren and himself, the liberty to act according to the dictates of conscience, in regard to things in themselves indifferent. And as appears, after he had been compelled to take refuge by flight to New England, he declared here, and the declaration was sent over to England to be published there, "I speak not against the doctrine of faith of the Church of England; for we are to bless God, that hath given the king a heart to maintain it."* And it is to her disgrace that by the most relentless intolerance she drove forth, as a fugitive for life, one of her ministers so true to her creed, and so willing to serve her in the use of the eminent talents God had given him.

Under circumstances so trying, as those of interdiction from preaching a gospel which he loved, and which was the ground of all hope for salvation; a man having the elements of character united in Mr. Hooker, was a man to think intensely; to feel deeply; to inquire for duty conscientiously; to realize the dangers of the times, and to anticipate anxiously the scenes before him. Such a man, thus situated, was also one to pray fervently, for light, direction, help, safety; to task his own patience, prudence, judgment, intellect, to the utmost, in making his way to conclusions on duty, which should be so sound as to need no revision. Having done all these things, he was also the man to form pur-

---

* See his "Soul's Effectual Calling to Christ," p. 447.

poses, high and momentous to himself, and to those with whom he was to sympathize and act; and to carry out those purposes with the decision and moral courage becoming a man, a christian, and a christian minister.

For this day of trial, Mr. Hooker had been in the process of both intellectual and spiritual training, while in his retirement at Emmanuel college, and subsequently in his active ministry both at Chelmsford and in Holland. He had also, doubtless, attentively studied the book of Providence, which, in those trying times, was opening its pages to the eyes of the good men of England, from day to day. He had studied human nature, also, in the Church and in the State; as it exhibited itself in the king upon his throne, in the nobles in their halls, in the archbishops and bishops in their palaces, in their robes and on their high seats, in the judges upon the bench, and more than all, in the members of the Council Table, the Star Chamber, and the Court of High Commissions, occupying seats of influence and power, and carrying out their designs against all good Puritans, in the union of those two fearful instrumentalities, espionage and despotism.

Occupied with such subjects of study thus forced upon his attention, Mr. Hooker had been in a course of preparation for "the things which might befall him," in the field of public duty and action. He had come to the eventful period when his opinions and principles respecting civil and religious rights brought him into collision with the lords spiritual and judicial. It would be deeply interesting, could we get possession of some newly discovered manuscript from Mr. Hooker's pen, written between the years of his residence at Cambridge, and his flight to New England; and which could give us, the records of his thoughts and the workings of his mind, while he looked upon the hostile aspect of the Church and the State, before him. It would also be instructive, could we learn from the pages of such a diary, how he contemplated his duties to his king, his church, and his country, in connection with his duty to God, and how he sought relief at the throne of grace, from the solicitude and fear which must have agitated him. We should, doubtless, see how and where a good man finds support, when "his foes are the men of his own household."

Men like Mr. Hooker, when they live in such scenes, and have such questions of duty to weigh—when they have decisions to make, which involve not only their own, but the interests, spiritual and temporal, of generations yet unborn;

and especially when they have these decisions to make with reference to the final approbation of conscience and of God, in the last judgment, must pass through agitations and conflicts, through alternations of hope and fear, of confidence and of trembling, which can be rightly estimated by Him only who "seeth in secret," and who knows the heart of his people when they suffer "for righteousness sake."

Mr. Hooker's residence seems to have continued near Chelmsford, for some time after he was silenced. He employed himself meanwhile in teaching a school at Little Braddow, having John Eliot, afterwards "the apostle of the Indians," in his family as an usher. By his instructions to youth, at that period, he was instrumental in bringing forward several good ministers in subsequent years.

John Eliot, speaking of his residence with Mr. Hooker, says, "To this place I was called, through the infinite riches of God's mercy in Christ Jesus to my poor soul; for here the Lord said unto my dead soul, live; and through the grace of Christ I do live, and I shall live forever. When I came to this blessed family, I then saw and never before, the power of godliness, in its lively vigor, and efficacy."*

* Mag., vol. I, p. 305. Life of Eliot, p. 47.

This testimony speaks much; but it awakens the earnest wish that more could be known of the habits of family religion, which had place in Mr. Hooker's house. To know how such a man was accustomed to manage his religious intercourse with his family; to have descriptions of the morning and evening devotions; of the Sabbath occupations; of the habits of conversation, in which he promoted the spiritual good of his own family, and those who resided with him; would not merely gratify pious curiosity, but would, doubtless, do much to stimulate christian fidelity.

And yet, this man, at the time to which Mr. Eliot alludes, was under the interdict of the Bishop of London not to preach "the gospel of Christ." Not for any offence against the laws of Christ; not for defection from the truth; not for having in any way forfeited the character of "a good minister of Jesus Christ;" but for declining conformity to the injunction of the Established Church, upon its ministers, that they "*keep the unity of apparel*," being "*canonically habited, with a square cap, a scholar's gown, priest-like, a tippet, and in the Church a linen surplice.*" *

* Neal's Hist. Puritans, I, 98. Harper's Edit., 1843.

It availed him nothing that he could declare the doctrinal belief of the English Church to be his own. There was required of him a conformity to the outward and Popish "gear" of the Church; irrespective of any fidelity there might be in him to the faith of the church.

The sentence, silencing Mr. Hooker, was deeply regretted, even by many ministers of the Established Church. Forty-seven of them presented a petition to the Bishop of London, on his behalf; in which they certified, "that they knew Mr. Hooker to be orthodox in his doctrine, honest in his life and conversation, peaceable in his disposition, and in no wise turbulent or factious." This testimony, though coming from churchmen and clergymen, and touching every point on which reasonable men in the higher offices of the church would insist, availed nothing. The bishop's seal was upon his lips, and he was compelled to be silent, as to the public duties of the ministry.

It was, however, impossible that he should refrain from all efforts to do good, and to exert the influence of a lover of truth and godliness, around him. It is related of him that he engaged the various ministers in the vicinity of Chelmsford, to establish a monthly meeting for fasting, prayer, and religious conference. By

4*

his influence, several pious young ministers were settled in the neighborhood, and others became more established in the fundamental doctrines of the gospel.*

To the injunction of the spiritual court against Mr. Hooker's preaching the gospel, was added a bond, in the sum of £50, to appear before the Court of High Commission. By the advice of his friends, he forfeited his bond, rather than expose himself to the hazards of appearing before a court so notoriously despotic, and relentless; and from which, he would doubtless have passed to prison, for years, if not for his whole life. One of his hearers, who was his surety, paid the bond; and was reimbursed by several good people in the vicinity of Chelmsford. After a short residence in retirement, kindly and courteously provided for him by his friend the Earl of Warwick, he left the country for Holland.† The

* Brooke's Lives of the Puritans, III, 65.

† The fact appears in the life of Rev. Henry Whitfield, that though himself a conformist, for twenty years, "yet a pious non-conformist was all this time very dear to him, and such persecuted servants of Christ, as Mr. Cotton, Mr. Hooker, Mr. Goodwin, and Mr. Page, then molested for their non-conformity, were sheltered under his roof." It does not appear at what time Mr. Hooker was thus hospitably entertained and protected by Mr. Whitfield, though it doubtless was the fact that in his numerous flights, from the pursuivants of the church, he, at some time, took refuge in his house.

spirit of persecution, however, which had taken away his office, and imposed an unrighteous and heavy bond, was too intolerant even to allow him to leave the country in peace. Down to the moment of his embarkation, his steps were watched by the pursuivants of that church, which should have loved and protected him. He barely escaped their hands at the time of his sailing for Amsterdam. His passage was a perilous one. But he who commanded the wind and the waves, and who had yet a great work for him to do, for the cause of truth and godliness, brought him safe to his destined port.

Mr. Hooker seems to have been a man of strong faith, in times of danger; whether the danger was from the machinations of wicked men, or from the raging of the elements. When, at his departure for Holland, leaving his friends, and flying before the pursuivants who were in quest of him, one of them said, "Sir, what if the wind should not be fair, when you come to the vessel?" he simply replied, "Brother let us leave that with Him who keeps the wind in the hollow of his hand." And it is remarkable that the wind changed from a contrary to a favorable direction, as soon as he had arrived on board the ship. When the ship, on its passage, ran upon a shelf of sand, in the night, and they were in danger of shipwreck; Mr. Hooker, with a confidence not unlike that of Paul, on his voyage to Rome, assured his fellow voyagers that they should be preserved; and he was not disappointed.

Mr. Hooker's residence in Holland was of three years' continuance. His first labors in the ministry, in that country, were as an assistant of Mr. Paget, at Amsterdam. The term of his ministerial services here, however, was short. Mr. Paget exerted his influence, in the Classis, against Mr. Hooker, on the ground that he was suspected of favoring the Brownists; a sect who denied the Church of England to be a true church; and her ministers to be rightly ordained.*

No explanations, however, of his views on the subject, ever given by Mr. Hooker; nor any exculpations of himself from that charge, satisfied Mr. Paget. It appears, moreover, that Mr. Paget regarded with like jealousy Mr. Davenport, Mr. Ames, Mr. Forbes, and others. Mr. Hooker was not the man to desire association with a minister whose prejudices were so invincible as those of Mr. Paget; nor to preach to a congregation who sympathized so strongly

* Neal, I, 149.

in the jealousies of their pastor. He therefore quietly withdrew; removed to Delft, and became associated with the Rev. Mr. Forbes, an aged and excellent Scotch minister. Mr. Forbes "esteemed him highly, in love, for his works' sake;" and the harmony in which they lived as co-laborers, was both to their own honor as christian ministers, and to the comfort of the people. The congregation to which they preached was composed principally of English merchants, established at Delft. Mr. Hooker continued with Mr. Forbes two years; and then upon a call to Rotterdam to assist the Rev. Dr. William Ames, who had fled to Holland from the persecutions of Bishop Bancroft, he removed to that place. In addition to his labors in preaching, he assisted Dr. Ames in the preparation of his book, entitled, "Afresh Suit against Human Ceremonies in God's Worship." The esteem in which he was held by Dr. Ames was such as to lead the latter to say of him, "that notwithstanding his acquaintance with many scholars of different nations, he had never met with a man equal to Mr. Hooker, as a preacher or as a learned disputant."

Mr. Hooker's experience of the trials attendant on his ministry in England, had fitted him to be a sagacious and safe counselor upon all questions which concerned the instituted worship of God. His worth, in this respect, was highly appreciated by the learned and venerable Ames. The regards of Dr. Ames were fully reciprocated by Mr. Hooker, in the estimate which he formed and expressed respecting his works; especially his "Medulla Theologiae," and his "Casus Conscientiae;" which Mr. Hooker regarded as of a character so elementary, in matters of religious faith and practice, that, joined with the thorough knowledge of the Scriptures, they were almost sufficient, without the aid of any other theological works, to be the sole text books for theological study.

Although Mr. Hooker found many things in Holland pleasant to him, as a minister of the gospel; especially the liberty there enjoyed, to "preach the unsearchable riches of Christ;" he still felt that he could not invite his friends in England, who were suffering under ecclesiastical restriction and oppression, to come there with the purpose of establishing themselves. The state of religion in the churches in Holland, moreover, appears to have discouraged the idea of making it his own permanent residence, or advising any of his English friends to do so. And "God having provided some better thing" for both him and them; and reserving them as a seed with which to plant the gospel in the new western world; he was kept in the frame of mind indicated in that text of Scripture, "Arise ye and depart, for this is not your rest."

His feelings, at this time, are best indicated in a letter which he wrote from Rotterdam, to Mr. Cotton, apparently in a time of sickness and considerable perplexity.

"The state of these provinces, to my weak eye, seems wonderfully ticklish and miserable. For the better part,—heart religion,—they content themselves with very forms, though much blemished; but 'the power of godliness,' for aught I can see or hear, they know not. And if it were thoroughly pressed, I fear lest it would be fiercely opposed.

"My ague yet holds me. The ways of God's Providence, wherein he has walked towards me, in this long time of my sickness, and wherein I have drawn forth many wearyish hours, under his Almighty hand, (blessed be his name,) together with pursuits * and banishments,—which have waited upon me as one wave follows another,—have driven me to an amazement: his paths being too secret and 'past finding out' by such an ignorant, worthless worm as myself. I

* *i. e.*, Persecutions in his native land.

have looked over my heart and life, according to my measure, aimed and guessed as well as I could; and entreated His Majesty to make known his mind, wherein I missed; and yet, methinks, I cannot spell out readily the purpose of his proceedings; which, I confess, have been wonderful in miseries, and *more* than wonderful in mercies to me and mine."

There is, in this letter, a singular blending of the sorrows of a tender spirit, with the strong confidence of a son of adoption in his heavenly Father. And his concluding testimony to the divine mercies, as so greatly overbalancing all his afflictions, is most touching; and effectually rebukes that spirit of despondency and complaining, which, even in the christian, sometimes exclaims, "All these things are against me."

While Mr. Hooker was in Holland, the emigration of the oppressed and persecuted Puritans was rapidly going forward, from England to New England. Among them were many of his friends, who had resided in the county of Essex. The hearts which were sighing for the liberty which the Lord Jesus Christ has designed for his people, and, in all ages, has taught them to love, were in the condition indicated by the prophet, when he said, "Oh that I had in the wilderness a lodging-place;" and by the mourning David, when he said, "Oh that I had wings like a dove! for then would I fly away and be at rest. Lo, then I would wander far off and remain in the wilderness."

The objects contemplated by Mr. Hooker's friends, in removing to New England,—in accordance with those of the multitudes of other devoted men and women who were making their way hither every year,—were, "opportunity to enjoy and practice the pure worship of the Lord Jesus Christ, in churches gathered according to his direction." Those who wished to remove to New England for such purposes, and who had known Mr. Hooker during the period of his ministry in Essex, very naturally directed their eyes to him, as their minister, to emigrate with them, and to renew among them the work of instruction, through which they had been so richly profited in the earlier years of his ministry. In the state of depression, perplexity and darkness as to the future, which we have seen described in his letter to Mr. Cotton, the invitation which his Essex friends gave him to accompany them to New England, must have been to his heart in sweet fulfillment of that text of Scripture, "Unto the upright there ariseth light in the darkness." It showed him a way out of his troubles, plain, direct, immediate, and which could not be mistaken. With gratitude and holy confidence, he took the path thus opened. The sequel will show how he found on that path consolation, relief, joy, and prosperous usefulness as a minister of Christ.

His first steps, however, from Holland to New England, were to be taken amidst dangers at the hands of his persecutors in his native country. It appeared necessary that he should go to England on his way to New England. When, therefore, he once more set his face towards his native land, he could say, as did Paul, when going up to Jerusalem, "not knowing the things which shall befall me there;" and he might have added, "bonds and imprisonments abide me." The pursuivants of the church, as already stated, had followed him when he left England for Holland, to the very moment of his sailing; so that he but just escaped their hands. He knew that if, on his return, they did not meet him on the same spot whence he had sailed three years before, and shut him up in prison with the hundreds and thousands of others who were suffering "persecution for righteousness sake," it would be because his omnipresent Lord was watching over him, and holding him by his right hand.

The pursuivants were upon his track again, shortly after his arrival in England; and he found himself—even in the land of his fathers—hunted "like a partridge upon the mountains." They traced him to the house of his friend Rev. Samuel Stone, who was to be his associate in emigrating to New England. Mather's graphic account of the scene, and of Mr. Hooker's escape at that critical moment, will best tell the story.* When the pursuivants knocked at the door of the very chamber in which Mr. Hooker was in conversation, "Mr. Stone was at that instant smoking of tobacco; for which Mr. Hooker had been reproving him, as being then used by few persons of sobriety. Being also of a sudden and pleasant wit, he (Mr. Stone) stepped to the door, with his pipe in his mouth, and such an air of speech and look as gave him some credit with the officer. The officer demanded whether Mr. Hooker was not there? Mr. Stone replied, with a braving sort of confidence, '*What* Hooker? Do you mean Hooker that lived once at Chelmsford?' The officer answered, '*Yes, he!*' Mr. Stone, with a diversion like that which once helped Athanasius, made this true answer: 'If it be he you look

* Magnalia I, 309.

for, I saw him about an hour ago, at such a house in the town; you had best hasten thither after him.' The officer took this for a sufficient account, and went his way."

This incident plainly showed to Mr. Hooker that "Satan desired to have him;" and that he must look well to his steps if he hoped ever to see New England. He therefore studied concealment, during the rest of his brief sojourn in England.

The precise length of time which he spent in his native land, after his return from Holland, does not appear; nor is the manner in which he occupied himself known, or even the place where he resided. He took his departure from the Downs about the middle of July, in 1633, in the ship Griffin.* Among his fellow passengers were his choice friends, Mr. Cotton and Mr. Stone. And such was the danger of being pursued and arrested, that Mr. Hooker and Mr. Cotton were under the necessity of continuing incognito till the ship was well out upon the main ocean. They could not till then even take their turns in the public worship, daily held aboard ship. The religious services were at first, therefore, conducted by Mr. Stone, the

* Savage's Winthrop, I, 108.

only one who was known to the ship's company as a preacher.

The feelings with which Mr. Hooker left England seem to have been somewhat like those of the prophet Jeremiah, when hated and threatened by his countrymen. It appears that he preached, somewhere, a "farewell sermon" to England; whether while enjoying the safety of his ship, on her way across the Atlantic, or after his arrival in New England, is uncertain. His mind was in an unusual state of elevation. He uttered himself, as we learn from some imperfect, and, as one writer remarks, "injurious" notes, which were published, in strains both touching and prophetic. The extracts which follow are all which will be here given:

"It is not gold and prosperity which makes God to be our God. There is more gold in the West Indies than there is in all Christendom; but it is God's ordinances, in the virtue of them, that show the presence of God."

"Is not England ripe? Is she not weary of God? Nay she is fed for the slaughter."

"England hath seen her best days, and now evil days are befalling us."

"And thou, England, which hath been lifted up to heaven with means, shall be abased and brought down to hell; for if the mighty works which have been done in thee, had been done in India or Turkey, they would have repented ere this."

It appears not to have been in the spirit of denunciation that Mr. Hooker thus expressed himself, but of apprehension of her coming woes, as under the chastisement of him who "thresheth the nations in anger" for their sins. To suppose that this good man cherished any other feelings in what he uttered, would do him great injustice, by ascribing to him a state of mind altogether inconsistent with his character and habits of speech and of spirit, during all the years of his life, as an Englishman and a Christian. Some utterances have been imputed to him, which are too questionable to admit the belief that he ever used them. A sermon on "The Danger of Desertion," said to be his, and given in a recent work on Congregational history, bears some marks of authenticity; but many marks also of having been taken and published by an unfriendly or an unskillful stenographer.* It does not compare well, in matter, style, or spirit, with his published writings.—And while it is quite possible that Mr. Hooker did preach a sermon in some respects like this,

* Hanbury's Historical Memorials, vol. I, p. 492 and C.

we should do him injustice to call this his veritable farewell sermon.

That his solicitude respecting the land of his fathers was deep and abiding, appears, however, from expressions which fell from his lips, several years after his removal to this country. He evidently had studied the rebukes which the Scriptures address to nations on account of their sins, "trembling at the words of the God of Israel," and fearing both the provocation of divine judgments, and their infliction upon his native land.

It is interesting to observe how Mr. Hooker and his brethren and the good people sailing with them, after they were safely on their way, enjoyed and used their religious liberty during their voyage. They literally preached and prayed during the whole time of their flight from England to New England. By one or another of these three divines there was a sermon preached every day, while they were on board; indeed they had three sermons, or expositions, for the most part, every day; from Mr. Cotton in the morning, Mr. Hooker in the afternoon, Mr. Stone after supper in the evening.* Their Father and their God seemed

* Magnalia, Book III.

saying to them, as a portion of his Zion, in their little bark on the wide ocean, "Here will I dwell. I will satisfy her poor with bread; I will also clothe her priests with salvation and her saints shall shout aloud for joy."

The removal of Mr. Hooker from England was felt by good men who remained there, as an afflictive providence. Thomas Shepard, in giving the reasons for his own subsequent removal to New England, assigns as his third:—"I saw the Lord departed from England, when Mr. Hooker and Mr. Cotton were gone; and I saw the hearts of most of the godly set and bent that way, and I did think I should feel many miseries if I stayed behind."* There was perhaps too much of despondency in this observation of Mr. Shepard; but it was a testimony, both fraternal and honorable, of the esteem and reverence in which he held Mr. Hooker and Mr. Cotton.

Dr. Ames had intended following Mr. Hooker soon after his removal from Rotterdam. But death removed him to "a better country, even an heavenly." His widow and children afterwards came to New England, and experienced the kind offices of Mr. Hooker as their patron and friend in a new country.†

---

* Life of Shepard.

† Holmes' Hist., Camb., p. 40 in Mass. Hist. Col., vol. VII.

It should here be stated that "Mr. Hooker's company," so called, which afterwards constituted his church at Cambridge, had preceded him.* Their names are preserved among the records of the proprietors of Cambridge.†

---

* Savage's Life of Winthrop, I, 88, note.

† See Appendix A of this volume.

## CHAPTER III.

Mr. Hooker's arrival at Boston Welcome by friends preceding him. Character of the Puritan Christians then gathered in New England. Preparation for his new resi dence and sphere of influence. Settlement at Cambridge, and labors as a Minister. Discussion with Roger Williams. Epistle respecting the Cross in the Banners. Es timate in which he was held by the General Court of Massachusetts Bay. Various public labors.

Mr. Hooker and his associates arrived at Boston, on September 4th, 1633, after a voyage of six weeks.

The author of the "Wonder-working Providence of Zion's Saviour in New England," in his notices of events in that year, gives this record: "Behold the sea also bringing in whole ship-loads of mercies, more being filled with fresh forces for furthering this wonderfull worke of Christ, and indeed this yeare came in many pretious ones, whom Christ in his grace hath made much use of in these his churches, and commonwealth, insomuch that these people were even almost over-ballanced with the great income of their present possessed mercies, yet they addresse themselves to the sea-shore, where they courteously welcome the famous servant of Christ, grave, godly, and judicious Hooker, and the honoured servant of Christ, Mr. John Haynes, as also, the Reverend and much desired Mr. John Cotton, and the retoricall Mr. Stone, with divers others of the sincere servants of Christ, comming with their young, and with their old, and with their whole substance, to do him service in this Desart wildernesse. Thus this poore people have tasted liberally of the salvation of the Lord every way, they deeme it high time to take up the cup of thankfulnesse, and pay their vowes to the most high God, by whom they were holpen to this purpose of heart, and accordingly set apart the 16 day of October, (which they call the eighth Moneth, not out of any humour of singularity, as some are ready to censor them with, but of purpose to prevent the Heathenish and Popish observation of Dayes, Moneths, and Yeares, that they may be forgotten among the people of the Lord,) this day was solemnly kept by all the seven churches, rejoicing in the Lord, and rendering thanks for all their benefits."*

To Mr. Hooker this was an arrival among friends, most grateful to his heart as a Christian minister and a man of strong attachments.

* Mass. Hist. Col., XIII, pp. 184, 185.

We who live at this day of religious freedom can scarcely realize what intense joy he and other Puritan ministers and private Christians felt, in view of the contrast between their condition at the moment they landed in New England and that in which they had spent so many dark and anxious years in England. Here was the "liberty of the sons of God," so far as it can be experienced on this side heaven. To Mr. Hooker himself, who had for three years been an exile from his country, and, when he at last ventured to return, was obliged to look carefully lest he should fall into the hands of the pursuivants of the English church, and be lodged in a prison, the contrast must have been peculiarly delightful.

It is now our pleasure to contemplate this good man in the new scenes and circumstances in which he was to act. He is three thousand miles from the palace of his persecutor, Bishop Laud, and with "none to molest or make him afraid." He is surrounded by friends, some of whom came with him, and others who came before him. Besides his fellow voyagers, Cotton, Stone and Haynes, there were Winthrop, Wilson, Eliot, and others like them in goodly number, who had preceded him; each one of whom, as the men of Succoth said of the brethren of the valiant Gideon, "resembled the children of a king." And of those who, with these men for their leaders, had been congregating in New England for several years, it might be said, as of Israel, when they came up out of Egypt, "there was not one feeble person among their tribes." As a body of men, the Puritan settlers in Massachusetts Bay at that time, present to the student of history such a spectacle as had never before been seen since apostolic times. The annals of nations will not soon tell of an equal number of men having among them more sterling worth or weight of character, nor men better qualified than they to lay the foundations of a free state and of free churches. They came destined by Divine Providence to people a land where the experiment of a people governing themselves by laws of their own making, and by public servants of their own choice, and worshiping God according to the dictates of their own consciences, should be tried on an extensive scale. And when we have said these things of the New England forefathers, we have spoken of character, to the moral excellence and aggregate of which, Thomas Hooker made a contribution in his own person, not surpassed by any other man whose name is found in the catalogue of the Pilgrims.*

We have already seen that Mr. Hooker was well trained, intellectually, morally, and spiritually, and had learned, amidst the agitations of his country, "what constitutes a State," and what a Church; what may be the disorders and the dangers of both; and by contrast, what are the principles and forms of government best adapted to secure the ends for which they are created. He was now prepared to lend his aid in founding and constructing the institutions of a country which heaven had decreed should be free. We see him on New England ground, ready for the service of "Christ and the church," and ready also to do all that might properly be done by a Christian minister to promote the civil as well as religious interests of the country. He was welcomed in a manner which must have been most grateful to his feelings, and by numbers who had known and appreciated his ministry in the father-land. And it was certain that in him the New England colonies had an accession of no common value to their welfare, both temporal and spiritual.

* Mr. Hooker was "admitted a freeman," May 14, 1634, at the same time with Gov. Haynes, Cotton, Mayhew, and Stone.—Savage's Winthrop, II, 152, note.

At a fast, observed by the church at Newtown, afterwards called Cambridge, October 11, 1633, Mr. Hooker was chosen pastor and Mr. Stone teacher. This church was the eighth gathered in the colony of Massachusetts Bay,* and this was their first choice of ministers. Mr. Hooker received ordination again, at the hands of his brethren, on his entrance upon office at Cambridge, although he had received ordination by a bishop as a presbyter in England.† He thus within the short space of five weeks after his arrival in New England, became the pastor of a Congregational church, and entered upon the work he so much loved among a people who were prepared to "rejoice in his light."

It mattered little to men of the spirit of Hooker, Cotton, and others of their associates, that after their departure Heylyn and other wits followed them with their "ungodly ribaldry," calling them "the bell-wethers" of the flocks, which had gone to New England, and making them and their religion the subjects of their ballads, for the diversion of the thoughtless and profane.‡ That all sorts of weapons should have been brought into service by the enemies

* Mass. Hist. Col., XV. 136.

† Mass. Hist. Col., VII, 39.

‡ See Hanbury, II. 40. 11.

of Puritanism, was to be expected. And when persecution had driven them across the Atlantic, there was of course leisure for ballad-mongers to employ their powers at the expense of good men, of whom the authorities of the establishment had succeeded in ridding the country.—"Behold their sitting down and their rising up; I am their music," said the author of Lamentations.* "And now am I their song, yea I am their byword," said Job of those that reproached him.† "And I was the song of the drunkards," said the devout King of Israel.‡ It was, however, immeasurably less a reproach to Bishop Laud's exiles that they should be thus celebrated, than it was to that church in whose service, for Christ's sake, they had been willing to spend their lives, that she should have had such helpers in "casting out their names as evil."

It is here in place to notice the reasons assigned by Mr. Cotton for his own and Mr. Hooker's removal to New England, as given in a letter by the former, apparently to some brother yet remaining in England. The letter bears date, Boston, December 3, 1634, more than a year after their arrival in this country. The following extract will be sufficient for the purpose.

* 3: 63. † Job 30: 9. ‡ Ps. 69: 12.

"The questions you demand, I had rather answer by word of mouth, than by letter, yet I will not refuse to give you account of my brother Hooker's removal and of mine own, seeing you require a reason thereof from us both. We both of us concur in a threefold ground of removal.

"1. God having shut a door against both of us from ministering to him and his people in our wonted congregations, and calling us by a remnant of our people, and by others of this country to minister to them here, and opening a door to us this way, who are we that we should strive against God and refuse to follow the concurrence of his ordinance and providence together, calling us forth to minister here. If we may and ought to follow God's calling three hundred miles, why not three thousand?

"2. Our Saviour's warrant is in our case, that when we are distressed in our course in one country (nequid dicam gravius) we should flee to another. To choose rather to bear witness to the truth by imprisonment than by banishment, is indeed sometimes God's way, but not in case men have ability of body and opportunity to remove, and no necessary engagement for to stay. Whilst Peter was young he might gird himself and go whither he would. John 21: 8, but when he was old and unfit for travel, then God called him rather to suffer himself to be girt of others, and led along to prison, and to death. Nevertheless in this point I conferred with the chief of our people, and offered them to bear witness to the truth I had preached, and practiced amongst them even unto bonds, if they conceived it might be any confirmation to their faith and patience; but they dissuaded me from that course, as thinking it better for themselves, and for me, and for the church of God, to withdraw myself from the present storm, and to minister in this country to such of their town as they had sent before hither, and such others as were willing to go along with me, or to follow after me.

* * * * * *

What service myself and brother Hooker might do to our people or other brethren in prison (especially in close prison as was feared) I suppose we both of us (by God's help) do the same, and much more, and with more freedom from hence, as occasion is offered; besides all our other service to the people here, which yet is enough and more than enough to fill both our hands, yea the hands of many brethren more, such as yourself, should God be pleased to make way for your comfortable passage to us. To have tarried in England for the end you mention, to appear in defence of that cause for which we were questioned, had been (as we conceive it in our case) to limit witness-bearing to the cause (which may be done in more ways than one) to one only way, and that such a way as we do not see God calling us unto. Did not Paul bear witness against the Levitical ceremonies, and yet chose rather to depart quickly out of Jerusalem, because the most of the Jews would not receive his testimony concerning Christ in that question (Acts 22: 18,) than to stay at Jerusalem to bear witness to that cause unto prison and death? Not that we came hither to strive against ceremonies (or to fight against shadows) there is no need of our further labor in that course; our people here desire to worship God in spirit and in truth, and our people left in England know as well the grounds and reasons of our suffering against these things, as our sufferings themselves, which we beseech the Lord to accept and bless, in our blessed Saviour. How far our testimony there hath prevailed with any others, to search more seriously into the cause, we do rather observe in thankfulness and silence, than speak of to the prejudice of our brethren.

"3. It hath been no small inducement to us, to choose rather to remove hither, than to stay there, that we might enjoy the liberty, not of some ordinances of God, but of all, and all in purity. For though we bless the Lord with you for the gracious means of salvation, which many of your congregations do enjoy (whereof our own souls have found the blessing, and which we desire may be forever continued, and enlarged to you) yet seeing Christ hath instituted no ordinance in vain (but all to the offering of the body of Christ) and we know that our souls stand in need of all to the utmost; we durst not so far be wanting to the grace of Christ, and to the necessity of our own souls, as to sit down somewhere else under the shadow of some ordinances, when by two months travel we might come to enjoy the liberty of all."*

Mr. Hooker was influential with Mr. Richard Mather, in persuading him to come to New England. In a letter to Mr. Mather on this subject, he said, "If I speak my own thoughts freely and fully, though there are many places where men may expect and obtain greater worldly advantage; yet I do believe there is not a place upon the face of the earth where a person of a judicious head and a generous heart may receive greater spiritual good to himself, and do more spiritual and temporal good to oth-

* Hutchinson's Mass. Bay, vol. III, pp. 55. 56, 57.

ers." This encouragement from Mr. Hooker brought to this country the father and ancestor of that family of good men, whose names have stood so prominent in the ecclesiastical history of New England. Through the instrumentality of Mr. Cotton and Mr. Hooker, Mr. Mather shortly after his arrival, became the pastor of the church in Dorchester, Massachusetts.

The influence of two such master minds as Mr. Hooker and Mr. Cotton, in the ecclesiastical affairs of Massachusetts, began to be felt soon after their arrival.

"Those that came over soon after Mr. Endicott, viz., Mr. Higginson and Mr. Skelton, Anno 1629, walked something in an untrodden path; therefore it is the less to be wondered at, if they went but in and out; in some things complying too much, in some things too little, with those of the separation; and it may be in some things not sufficiently attending to the order of the gospel, as themselves thought they understood afterwards. For in the beginning of things they only accepted of one another, according to some general profession of the doctrine of the gospel, and the honest and good intentions they had one toward another, and so by some kind of covenant, soon moulded themselves into a church in every plantation, where they took up their abode; until Mr. Cotton and Mr. Hooker came over, which was in the year 1633, who did clear up the order and method of church government, according as they apprehended was most consonant to the word of God."*

The history of the period of Mr. Hooker's ministry at Cambridge, is not marked by many events or transactions of importance aside from the usual duties of a diligent and faithful pastor and teacher. He had not come to New England in pursuit of adventures, or to do things which should make him famous among his countrymen. He had come to preach the unsearchable riches of Christ; to live himself, and to assist others to live, in holiness; and to prepare for heaven. Moreover he needed quietness and rest, such as consisted with his beloved work as an "ambassador for Christ." And his Lord and Master mercifully gave him, during his first years in New England, a season of rest. And in this, as it now appears, he was in preparation for arduous and responsible labors, both as a Christian minister, and a member of the body politic, with which he filled up the concluding period of his life.

Mr. Hooker gave himself diligently to his

* Hubbard's Hist. in Mass. Hist. Coll., XV. 181, 182

work among the people of his own pastoral charge; and took a prominent part with the other ministers of Massachusetts Bay, in whatever was to be done to give stability and strength to the church and to the Colony. Winthrop notes his association with Warham, Cotton, and Welde, in the maintenance of a weekly Thursday Lecture in Boston, Cambridge, Dorchester, and Roxbury.

"October 5. It being found that the four lectures did spend too much time, and proved over burdensome to the ministers and people; the ministers with the advice of the magistrates, and with consent of their congregations, did agree to reduce them to two days, viz., Mr. Cotton at Boston on Thursday or the 5th day of the week, and Mr. Hooker at Newtown the next 5th day, and Mr. Warham at Dorchester one 4th day of the week, and Mr. Welde at Roxbury the next 4th day."* Richly must these good men have enjoyed the privileges of a ministry exercised under no other constraints than the holy fear of God and the love of Christ.

In 1634 Mr. Hooker was the preacher before the General Court, held at Cambridge. We find him in 1633, associated with Haynes, and

* Savage's Winthrop, vol. I, p. 144.

in 1635, with Cotton and Wilson in consultation for the purpose of reconciling some differences between Governor Winthrop and Lieutenant Governor Dudley, in regard to the manner of administering the government of the Colony ;* Winthrop having been in favor of leniency adapted to their circumstances as an infant colony; and Dudley being in favor of more strictness. The result of their consultation was such as might have been expected, from the efforts of such men, prayerfully devoting themselves to the work of peace-making.

In 1634, Mr. Hooker was also associated with Mr. Cotton and Mr. Welde, by desire of the Assistants, in a conference with Mr. John Eliot, respecting a sermon in which he had taken occasion to speak against a peace made with the Pequods. The result of the conference was that Mr. Eliot was brought to acknowledge his error, and to make a public retraction of it on the next Lord's day.†

In this year, also, Mr. Hooker was called to the experience of severe domestic affliction, in the loss of a young son, by the small-pox.‡

Toward the conclusion of the period of Mr.

* Savage's Winthrop, I, 117, 118, 177.

† Mass. Hist. Coll. VIII. 29; and Savage's Winthrop, I. 151.

‡ Savage's Winthrop, I. 385.

Hooker's residence in Massachusetts bay, he was engaged in a discussion, before the General Court, with Mr. Roger Williams, respecting his peculiar views; which had created no small excitement in the colony. The occasion was this: Mr. Williams appeared before the General Court and the assembled ministers of the commonwealth. He was inquired of respecting certain letters; in one of which he had made complaints to the churches against the magistrates; and in another, addressed to his own church, had endeavored to persuade them to renounce communion with the other churches. In the presence of this body of men, "Mr. Hooker was appointed to dispute with Mr. Williams."* Although the result of the discussion between the two men was not such as had been desired, the fact that Mr. Hooker, without any previous notice apparently, was designated, on the part of the General Court and the ministers of Massachusetts bay, to enter the arena of disputation with "Roger Williams," indicates the confidence with which they relied upon Mr. Hooker's intellectual power and ready skill in public debate. He appears, on this occasion, not as a lover of controversy, but in the performance of

* Mass. Hist. Coll. VIII. 17, note.

public duty, assigned to him by men to whose wishes it became him to show respect, even though at the sacrifice of his own preference to remain silent.

At about this period, there arose considerable disturbance in the colony of Massachusetts bay, from the cutting of the cross out of the military colors, at Salem. This was the act of Mr. Endicott, in his zeal against "anti-christian superstition."* The honesty of Mr. Endicott's intentions appears to have been unquestioned; and he seems to have supposed himself justified by some of Mr. Williams' preaching. He acted, however, without Mr. Williams' advice; and it does not appear that Mr. Williams ever justified the act, after it was done. Mr. Endicott thus brought himself into serious difficulty with the authorities of the colony.

In the library of the Massachusetts Historical Society is preserved a manuscript, by Mr. Hooker, "Touching the Crosse in the Banners." It is not found as published, in any of the historical memorials of New England; nor is it clear, from the paper itself, to whom it was addressed. Mr. Hooker's apology for writing at all upon the subject is contained in the following para-

* Knowles' Life of Roger Williams, p. 62.

graphs :—"That now I shall expresse myselfe (my witnesse in heaven) is not like of opposition to any man's person or opinion. For the Lord knoweth it is my affliction to differ in judgment from many of my faithful brethren, and most crosse to my inclination to expresse contrarily therein. But being importuned, publiquley and privately, by speech and letter, and that by some to whom I owe much in the Lord, and without whose invitation it was in my heartt never to put pen to paper on this point; conceiving myself thus constrained by call to expresse my sudden apprehensions, I shall crave leave, by way of inquisition only, to propose an argument or two.

"Not that I am a friend to the crosse as an idoll, or to any idollatry in it; or that any carnall fear takes me asyde and makes me unwilling to give way to the evidence of the truth, because of the sad consequences that may be suspected to flowe from it. I blesse the Lord, my conscience accuseth me of no such thing; but that as yet I am not able to see the sinfulness of this banner in a civil use. Those who see none, by grace received, and to whom the Lord is pleased to give a more speedy discerninge of things propounded to them, must not take it ill, if these who have been long settled in some principles, (which they conceive to be truth,) are heavy of apprehension to see through things objected, or yet to cleare their own thoughts, and, therefore, need and crave longer time of consideration before they can come to determine any thing."

The expression, "as yet I am not able to see the sinfulness of this banner in a civil use," presents the general view which Mr. Hooker took of the matter. He quietly goes on to justify this general view; presenting such suggestions as the following:—"1. It is requisite, yea necessary, that some banner be displayed in warre. 2. This banner, in a civil way, is as apt to attaine the aid in gatheringe and guidinge soldiers as any other. 3. Had it never been abused, idolatrously and superstitiously, then [there] had been no more question of using this than any other. 4. This abuse is that which is superadded to the civil use, namely, when it was impiously instituted and observed as a cause of protection from danger; or deliveringe men out of danger, then was it made an idoll, and set in the room of God, in whose hands protection and preservation only is. When, also, it was ordained and appointed as a moral or sacramental sighne, to draw or stirre the bearer to Christ in love or hope, then became it superstitious. This superstitious abuse, as it was superadded, so may it again be removed from the natural and civil use hereof, being only a separable adjunct."

The foregoing extracts, from the manuscript, are sufficient to show that Mr. Hooker had not been set on fire by this matter, and was not willing that the colony of Massachusetts Bay should be blown up into a popular blaze respecting it. Nor had he any disposition to involve himself in a controversy upon the subject with Mr. Williams, or his zealous and well-meaning friend, Mr. Endicott. The piece is worth publishing entire, did our limits permit, as exemplifying the union of a right and charitable temper, with "the spirit of wisdom," in a good man, for the arrest of contention, and the restoration of peace among men in commotion.

Cotton Mather, speaking of this excitement, says, "Some of our chief worthies maintained their different persuasions, with weapons, indeed, no worse than a little harmless and learned ink-shed." The biographer of Roger Williams gives Mr. Hooker the credit of having written "a tract of nearly thirteen pages in defence of the cross." The counsels of peace, it seems, prevailed. "The matter was finally settled, by leaving out the cross in the colors of the trained bands, and retaining it in the banner of the castle and of vessels."*

This little passage in the history of those times is of interest to us of the present day, as indicating, that from the first planting of the tree of liberty, civil and religious, in New England, it was a settled point that there never could be, for a moment, the least toleration here, of any thing which should be a symbol of Popery. The Puritans had seen enough of such things on the other side of the ocean. They loved "the cross of Christ," in the New Testament sense of that expression. But they neither wanted, nor, for a moment, would tolerate, any other than New Testament provisions and aids, for the guidance of their minds or the proper effecting of their hearts, in the contemplation of this great and glorious theme.

At no period of his life does Mr. Hooker appear to have courted controversy. Nevertheless, when it was required by the interests of christian truth and gospel order, he was ready for the discharge of his share of this duty.

With these last pieces of public service, Mr. Hooker closed his labors as a citizen and minister of Massachusetts Bay. The period of his

* Knowles' Life of Roger Williams, p. 63, note.

residence there had been a brief one. But it was filled up as became "a good minister of Jesus Christ," with labors abundant; and these performed with the spirit and fidelity of one "ready to every good work."

## CHAPTER IV.

Mr. Hooker's plan of removal, with his people, to Hartford. Discussion of the subject in the General Court. Reasons assigned. Other reasons, probable. Journey of the emigrating pastor and church to Hartford. Vindication of Mr. Hooker from certain misrepresentations of his reasons for the removal.

We now come to that important period in the life of Mr. Hooker, in which the plan for his emigration with his church from Cambridge to found a new colony upon Connecticut river originated; an event which resulted in the settlement of Hartford, and put in motion a train of events of high importance in the history of Connecticut, both as a State and a community of churches. In this enterprise, Mr. Hooker was the leader, as he had been the originator, and thus became one of the founders of the commonwealth.

It is quite natural to ask here, Why should Mr. Hooker remove from Newtown? Why leave the prosperous colony of Massachusetts Bay? The almost idolized pastor of his church, not all of whom might be able to remove with him; settled in pastoral comfort, and permanently, doubtless, if he so pleased; having strong, as well as numerous, inducements to remain, such as the excellent circle of ministerial society about him, the pleasant character and prosperous condition of the churches which had been planted in Boston, Dorchester, Roxbury, Watertown, Salem, and Lynn; having, also, reached the meridian of his life, the time to begin to think of its decline, and to plan for old age; under such circumstances, presenting strong inducements to remain in that goodly home, why should he break away, and travel through the wilderness more than a hundred miles, to settle in the vicinity of twelve or fifteen thousand Indians, besides many jealous and quarrelsome Dutchmen; and, with a company of one hundred men, women, and children, begin the planting of a new colony, and the construction, from the beginning, of a new order of things, both civil and ecclesiastical?

Puritans were not wont to be men of inexplicable movements. And Mr. Hooker, as we have seen, in all his history, up to this time, always had good reasons for his proceedings, and was ready to make them known, whenever it was necessary, for the satisfaction of his christian brethren.

This emigration to Hartford was not a hasty, or an ill-advised measure. The subject of a removal as a matter of imperious necessity, had been brought before the General Court of Massachusetts, in September, 1634; only one year subsequent to Mr. Hooker's arrival from England. And almost two years elapsed before the removal actually took place.

As the reasons for this movement, so far as Mr. Hooker was concerned, have been, and continue to this day, to be misunderstood by some, and misrepresented by others; it is proper and necessary to give here the authentic and impartial history of the discussions of the subject, and the measures which preceded the emigration, as given by Governor Winthrop:—

"September 4, [1634.] The General Court began at Newtown, and continued a week, and then was adjourned fourteen days. Many things were there agitated and concluded, as fortifying in Castle Island, Dorchester and Charlestown, also against tobacco, and costly apparel, and immodest fashions; and committees appointed for setting out the bounds of towns, with divers other matters which do not appear upon record. But the main business, which spent the most time, and caused the adjourning of the court, was about the removal of

Newtown. They had leave, the last general court, to look out some place for enlargement or removal, with promise of having it confirmed to them, if it were not prejudicial to any other plantation; and now they moved, that they might have leave to remove to Connecticut. This matter was debated divers days, and many reasons alledged pro and con. The principal reasons for the removal were,—1. Their want of accommodation for their cattle, so as they were not able to maintain their ministers, nor could receive any more of their friends to help them; and here it was alledged by Mr. Hooker, as a fundamental error, that towns were set so near to each other.

"2. The fruitfulness and commodiousness of Connecticut, and the danger of having it possessed by others, Dutch and English.

"3. The strong bent of their spirits to remove thither.

"Against these it was said,—1. That in point of conscience they ought not to depart from us, being knit to us in one body, and bound by oath to seek the welfare of this commonwealth.

"2. That in point of state and civil policy, we ought not to give them leave to depart. 1. Being we were now weak and in danger of being assailed. 2. The departure of Mr. Hooker would not only draw many from us, but also divert other friends that would come to us. 3. We should expose them to evident peril, both from the Dutch, (who made claim to the same river, and had already built a fort there,) and from the Indians, and also from our own state at home, who would not endure they should sit down without a patent in any place which our king lays claim unto.

"3. They might be accommodated at home by some enlargement which other towns offered.

"4. They might remove to Merrimack, or any other place within our patent.

"5. The removing of a candlestick is a great judgment, which is to be avoided.

"Upon these and other arguments, the court being divided, it was put to vote; and, of the deputies, fifteen were for their departure, and ten against it. The governor and two assistants were for it, and the deputy and all the rest of the assistants were against it, (except the secretary, who gave no vote;) whereupon no record was entered, because there were not six assistants in the vote, as the patent requires. Upon this grew a great difference between the governor and assistants and the deputies. They would not yield the assistants a negative voice, and the others, (considering how dangerous it might be to the commonwealth, if they should not keep that strength to balance the greater number of the deputies,) thought it safe to stand upon it. So, when they could proceed no further, the whole court agreed to keep a day of humiliation to seek the Lord, which was accordingly done, in all the congregations, the 18th day of this month; and the 24th the court met again. Before they began, Mr. Cotton preached, (being desired by all the court, upon Mr. Hooker's instant excuse of his unfitness for that occasion.) He took his text out of Hag. 2 : 4, &c., out of which he laid down the nature or strength (as he termed it) of the magistracy, ministry and people, viz.,—the strength of the magistracy to be their authority; of the people, their liberty; and of the ministry, their purity; and shewed how all these had a negative voice, &c., and that yet the ultimate resolution, &c., ought to be in the whole body of the people, &c., with answer to all objections, and a declaration of the people's duty and right to maintain their true liberties against any unjust violence, &c., which gave great satisfaction to the company. And it pleased the Lord so to assist him, and to bless his own ordinance, that the affairs of the court went on cheerfully; and, although, all were not satisfied about the negative voice to be left to the magistrates, yet no man moved aught about it, and the congregation of New-town came and accepted of such enlargement as had freely been offered them by Boston and Watertown; and so the fear of their removal to Connecticut was removed."*

The absolute necessity for the removal of Mr. Hooker and his church to some other place will farther appear from these considerations. The emigration of Hooker, Cotton, and Stone from England to New England, had given a new impulse to the spirit of emigration among the English Puritans, insomuch that multitudes now were every month arriving, to establish themselves here.† The country around Boston was as yet cleared only in moderate space for making settlements, and for the raising of crops and the sustenance of the inhabitants and their cattle. Moreover it was a matter of some delicacy for the first settlers, the moment their friends from England should set foot upon land, to advise them to plunge immediately into the wilderness of the interior in search of homes. It was far more in accordance with the spirit of Puritanism that there should be some sacrifice of present comfort and convenience, on the part of the ear-

* Savage's Winthrop, I. 140—142.

† Mass. Hist. Col., XV, 169.

lier and more experienced settlers in the vicinity of Boston, to accommodate the emigrants, who had yet to learn what it was to live in a new country.

As showing how great was the stream of emigration which was setting towards this country, a single fact will suffice. In a letter from Governor Winthrop to his son, dated "this 26 of the 2 mo 1636," he thus writes: "Mr. Hooker and his company intend to set forth three weeks hence." Directly under this sentence, in form of a postscript, he adds, "This night we hear of a ship arrived at Pemaquid, and of twenty-four ships upon the seas, bound hither." Such a piece of intelligence as this must have settled the question respecting the expediency of emigrating to Hartford, and brought them to the conclusion that somebody must remove in order to make room for the multitudes who were known to be on their way to New England.

The foresight and peaceable disposition of Mr. Hooker, moreover, led him to suggest the advice, that they "should not incur the danger of an Ezek or a Sitnah," (i. e., contention and hatred,) "when they might have a Rehoboth," (room, commodious and abundant space.)

Additional to these arguments for Mr. Hooker's removal with his church to Hartford, other probable reasons may be assigned, when we consider the man in his character and his obvious motives of action, and when also we look at him in his association with other Puritans, for the great purposes contemplated in their emigration to New England. Men like Hooker, Haynes, Stone, and Hopkins, in taking this step, in the face of all the objections urged by their brethren of the colony, and in view of all the perils of the wilderness, must have acted under higher and better impulses than those which regarded only their personal and private interests. They were Christian men, having made a high and determined consecration of themselves to the great interests of civil and religious liberty. We must believe that they were looking beyond the bound of their own brief lives to the results of their decisions and movements, as they could be anticipated by the sagacity of men living for the good of coming generations.

With reverence be it said, also, we believe that He "from whom all holy desires and all just counsels do proceed," had "put it into their hearts to fulfill his will," and to execute the plans suggested by his grace; plans which were to take deep hold upon the interests of a republic, destined, as now appears, to stretch itself from ocean to ocean, and to spread out to the north and to the south, through many degrees of latitude. We seem to see, in Hooker and his associates, while weighing the question of their removal, that which is sometimes seen in wise and good men, a forecast almost prophetic, under the influence of which they project plans and perform acts which take hold upon the future, almost as directly as if the God in whom they trusted had enabled them to look into futurity. Mr. Hooker was not an inspired prophet, but he had subjected his own mind to the Infinite Mind; he had put his hand into the hand of Him of whom it is written, "Thou leddest thy people like a flock, by the hand of Moses and Aaron." He appears to have perceived and obeyed some intimations of Providence, in the direction of the proposed scene of the new plantation, which other men around him had not observed. And it is a circumstance to make the people of Connecticut at this day to feel a satisfaction almost sacred, while they look back to the date of the pending question, and then follow the course of events for more than two hundred years, to the present time; while they remember why they are in so goodly a portion of this garden, New England, and what their commonwealth is in its great interests, social, civil, educational, and religious; and while they consider that the God of our fathers was leading this his tried and faithful servant in the way in which he would both bless him, and through his means bless them "in these last days."

This account of the reasons for the removal of Mr. Hooker and his people to Hartford has been necessary, that he may be vindicated against an imputation which appears in the histories of both Hubbard and Hutchinson,* and has, unfortunately, been countenanced in Robertson's history of America.† Robertson says: "The rivalship between Mr. Cotton and Mr. Hooker, two favorite ministers in the settlement of Massachusetts Bay, disposed the latter, who was the least successful in this contest for fame and power, to wish some settlement at a distance from a competitor by whom his reputation was eclipsed. A good number of those who had imbibed Mrs. Hutchinson's notions, and were offended at such as combated them, offered to accompany him."

If Mr. Hooker had such a reason for removing to Hartford, it is rather remarkable that it was not discovered in the course of the protracted discussion of this subject, which, as has been

* Hist. of Eng., 305, and Hist. Mass. Br., I, 43.

† Vol. I, p. 441.

already seen, arose in the General Court. That no such reason was discovered or believed to exist is quite certain, from the fact that Winthrop's history of the investigation gives not the slightest intimation of it. Moreover, the statement that some of Mrs. Hutchinson's followers proposed to follow Mr. Hooker to Hartford, so far from being true is utterly without foundation; for Mrs. Hutchinson's affairs were not publicly agitated till after Mr. Hooker's removal. Furthermore, Mr. Hooker was the last man in the whole circle of New England ministers from whom Mrs. Hutchinson and her followers could have expected any sympathy, for, as appeared subsequently, "this church as well as their minister, were more opposite to Mrs. Hutchinson and all the Antinomians than any church in Massachusetts.*

Besides all this, every thing which appears in New England history, respecting the intercourse of Mr. Hooker and Mr. Cotton, contradicts the imputation now under consideration, and goes to show that they were always upon terms of most fraternal and honorable friendship. They were companions in sufferings before they left England. They came to New England to-

* Eccl. Hist. Mass., p. 40.

gether. When inquired of why they left that country for this, they united in assigning their reasons. They took the freeman's oath together in this country. They were associated in the labors of the ministry. They were both philanthropists and lovers of civil and religious liberty. They were co-moderators of an assembly held at Cambridge, in consequence of an attempt to introduce Presbyterian government and discipline into the colony. And the names of no two men of their time, in the country, are more frequently mentioned together, as fraternally associated in the affairs of the churches, than the names of Hooker and Cotton.

Robertson is supposed to have derived his views of Hooker's motives from Douglass, who had vented a profusion of spleen upon the good people of New England, after a short residence among them, and whose reputation as a historian, for either candor or veracity, is not altogether enviable.* The testimony, therefore, of Governor Winthrop, a faithful and impartial historian, who was on the spot at the time, is preferable to that of two foreigners, three thousand miles off, who wrote under the obvious in-

---

* See Eccl. Hist. Mass., pp. 40, 41, note. Mr. Hutchinson's Mass. Br., I, 208, and II, 80.

fluence of prejudice against the Puritans of New England.

Of this important removal from Newtown to Hartford, the following account is given by Trumbull.*

"About the beginning of June, Mr. Hooker, Mr. Stone, and about a hundred men, women, and children, took their departure from Cambridge, and traveled more than a hundred miles, through hideous and trackless wildernesses, to Hartford. They had no guide but their compass; made their way over mountains, through swamps, thickets, and rivers, which were not passable but with great difficulty. They had no cover but the heavens, nor any lodgings but those which simple nature afforded them. They drove with them a hundred and sixty head of cattle, and by the way subsisted upon the milk of their cows. Mrs. Hooker was borne through the wilderness upon a litter. The people generally carried their packs, arms, and some utensils. They were nearly a fortnight on their journey. This adventure was the more remarkable, as many of this company were persons of figure, who had lived in England in honor, affluence, and delicacy, and entire strangers to fatigue and danger."

* Hist. Conn., I, 64, 65.

It is to be regretted that no one of the historians who have noticed this remarkable journey, has given any precise information respecting the route pursued from Newtown to Hartford. Hutchinson mentions "many hideous swamps and very high mountains, beside five or six rivers, or different parts of the same winding river, (the Chickapi,) not every where fordable, which they could not avoid."*

The "Chickapi" River was doubtless that which now bears the name *Chickopee*, rising in the vicinity of what is now Worcester, Massachusetts, pursuing a circuitous course through the towns now known as Spencer, Brookfield and Palmer, receiving on its way several tributary streams, large and small rising in New Braintree and Petersham, and a part of them constituting Ware and Swift rivers, and falling into the Connecticut above Springfield. Supposing the company of emigrants to have taken a direct course from Boston to what is now Spencer,—the place where they perhaps struck the Chickapi (or Chickopee) River,—they must have crossed the Charles and the Concord rivers and some smaller streams tributary to them.—Following the general course of the Chickopee,

---

* Hutchinson, I, 45.

they must have kept, most of their way, within the limits of Massachusetts, and approached the Connecticut not far from where Springfield now stands. Whether they crossed this river so high up, and passed down to Hartford upon the west side, or continued their journey on the east side till near the point at which they were aiming, is unknown. Tradition has spoken of the latter.*

In the condition of the country at that time, upon the route now described, and which was probably the one pursued, considered as a wilderness, without roads, bridges, or ferries; looking also at the number of the streams, and the size of some of them as they now are; and taking into the account the hills, valleys, swamps, ravines, all of them doubtless rendered the more forbidding from their being embraced in a wilderness; the conclusion will be natural, that a journey from Boston to Hartford, two hundred years ago, must have been attended with toils

* If the journey of the emigrants was upon the west side of the river, the observer of contrasts and student of modern "progress" will find matter for interesting comparison between a journey from Boston to Hartford in 1636 and one in 1849; the first requiring nearly a fortnight, at the rate of ten miles per day, and the second by rail-road along the same route, less than six hours from city to city.

and dangers hardly surpassed in these days, by a journey from the capital of Massachusetts across the continent of North America to the mouth of the Columbia River.

## CHAPTER V.

Arrival at Hartford. Share of Mr. Hooker in the concerns of the Colony of Connecticut superadded to his ministerial services. Cotemporaries and associates in the colonies of Connecticut. Estimate of his position and influence in the state. Concern in originating the New England Confederacy. Invitation to a seat in the Westminster Assembly of Divines, in England. Reasons for declining the invitation. Last sickness. Death. Letter of Mr. Stone relative to his decease.

We find Mr. Hooker and his church at "Hartford upon Connecticut," in June, 1636. He was there, too, for reasons which he needed not to be ashamed to see "written on the sky," to be read by all whom they might concern. Reasons they were which well became him, as a christian and a member of the civil state. He was there, to be with other wise and good men the founder of a state as well as of churches of Christ. And by his little colony of godly men, together with those of New Haven and of Saybrook, the erection of the good State of Connecticut that now is, was commenced. "History," says an eminent New England historian of our own time, "has ever celebrated the heroes who have won laurels in scenes of carnage. Has it no place for the founders of states; the wise legislators who struck the rock in the wilderness, so that the waters of liberty gushed forth in copious and perennial fountains? They who judge of men by their services to the human race, will never cease to honor the memory of Hooker and of Haynes."*

Mr. Hooker's Church, before their emigration to New England, had chosen Mr. Samuel Stone to be associated with him as a teacher. Mr. Stone's great excellence of character made him to be highly esteemed by them; and we find him continuing with Mr. Hooker and the church, in all their removals, and in that to Hartford. The fact speaks well, both for the ministers and their people. This happy union continued during the life of Mr. Hooker.

It is appropriate in the sketch of this period in the life of Mr. Hooker, that we speak of him, in this new field of his labors, not only as a Christian minister and pastor of the Church in Hartford, and in his ecclesiastical relations to the State, but also in his relations to the colony, and in his promotion of its interests, civil, literary, and moral.

---

* Bancroft's History of the United States, vol. I., p. 403.

The exigencies of that period in Connecticut were such as called for the counsels and coöperation of all men of intellectual force, education, prudence, sagacity, and moral courage; men capable of understanding the true interests of the colony; who could weigh difficult questions, and assist in settling first principles, so that they should not soon need revision. It was of the greatest importance that the ministers of the gospel should cordially coöperate with the civil fathers, as being men who could appreciate their just decisions, and second, with their approbation, all wise and efficient measures tending to the public welfare.

Whatever may be said respecting the inexpediency of Christian ministers engaging in civil and political life, in a settled condition of the country; it is evident that in the commencement of the work which our fathers undertook, men like Thomas Hooker, whether in the christian ministry or out of it,—men of intellect, heart, prudence, decision, efficiency,—had high responsibilities to civil society, and important duties to perform in the promotion of the best interests of the state. In relation to this subject, they had to choose between diligent coöperation with the civil fathers, on the one hand; and on the other, seclusion and inaction, amounting to treachery towards the state, and at the same time destructive to the christian ministry.

True, Mr. Hooker did not sustain precisely the relation to the colony of Connecticut which his friend Mr. Cotton did to that of Massachusetts ; a teacher in the pulpit, on the Sabbath, of principles of legislation which the General Court could embody in enactments during the following week. But his mind, opinions and counsels were influential in the more informal and social deliberations of wise and good men, upon the internal policy of the colony, and in the projection of its laws. Though not a member of the law-making body, that body had the benefit of his counsels in connection with those by whom they were proposed. "Though he did not appear to seek after civil appointments, yet such was the confidence of the General Court in his integrity and ability, that he was occasionally appointed upon important Committees. In 1639, Mr. Hooker and Mr. Wells were appointed by the General Court to consult with Mr. Fenwick "concerning the Bay's aiding in an offensive and defensive war ; * also relating

* In all probability, this, in Hooker's mind, was the germ of the New England Confederacy of 1643, of which notice will be taken in the sequel.

to the bounds of patents on Connecticut river. In 1640, he, together with Mr. Wells, was appointed to close a controversy which had long existed between Lieut. Robert Seeley and the plantation at Wethersfield. He received other appointments from the General Court." *

It is to the honor of the public men of that time, in Connecticut, who were employed in giving shape to civil institutions, that they were not at all infected with that absurd jealousy of the political influence of gospel ministers, which, in more recent times, has sought even to disfranchise every man who occupies a pulpit, for fear that he will either attempt the "union of Church and State," or use his privileges as a freeman and a minister to overturn "the State."

As Mr. Hooker's agency and influence in public and religious concerns, after his removal to Hartford, was somewhat prominent, some notices of his cotemporaries in the colonies which now constitute Connecticut, and a brief view of public affairs in his lifetime, will here be given; and the history of his course as a christian minister will then be resumed.

One of the "worthies" with whom Mr.

* Hinman's Catalogue of Early Settlers of Connecticut, p. 38.

Hooker acted, in the concerns of the colony of Connecticut, was EDWARD HOPKINS; styled by Cotton Mather, "the Solomon of his colony;" a man who added to his wisdom a high christian character and enlarged benevolence in action.

JOHN HAYNES, of the same colony, was the worthy compeer of Hopkins; if we judge from the fact, that for a considerable course of years he was chosen Governor of the colony, alternately with Hopkins.

GEORGE WILLYS, THOMAS WELLS, and JOHN WEBSTER, are styled by Mather, men of "wisdom, justice, and courage."

WILLIAM LEET was a man, like Daniel of old, of "an excellent spirit;" and was chosen Governor, after the union of the two colonies of New Haven and Connecticut.

THEOPHILUS EATON, Governor of the colony of New Haven, was a man of great discretion, gravity and equity; one whom Mather, borrowing from Luke's address, at the beginning of his gospel, styles, "most excellent Theophilus."

Rev. JOHN DAVENPORT was intimately associated with Eaton, and the two men have been styled, "the Moses and Aaron of the colony" of New Haven.

FRANCIS NEWMAN, of that colony, Mr. Eaton's successor in the office of Governor, was a man of the same style of character with him, having long been his associate.

ROBERT TREAT was like his predecessors, Eaton and Newman, in his general character, and was repeatedly called to office by the voice of the people.

JOHN WINTHROP, the second, son of the excellent Governor, of the same name, in Massachusetts Bay, and himself called very early in life into office, had much of the excellence which distinguished his honored father; "studious, humble, patient," a man of a great soul, as described by the author of Magnalia Americana.

Besides these, and more particularly associated with Mr. Hooker, in the colony of Connecticut, and several of them distributed in the towns of Hartford, Windsor and Wethersfield; were Ludlow, Watson, Whiting, Talcott, William Hopkins, Wolcott, Hull, Phelps, William Ludlow, Mason, Mitchell, Swain, Steele, Thurston, Haynes, Ward, Westwood, and Deming.

GEORGE FENWICK, though he did not long reside in the country, yet, while at Saybrook Plantation, he interested himself greatly in the welfare of the Hartford Church and their Pastor, and deserves a place among the worthies of the State. With him should be mentioned,

Gardiner, Peters, Leffingwell, Tracy, men of note at the mouth of Connecticut river; also the Huntingtons, Baldwins, Reynoldses, Backuses, Blisses, Watermans, Hydes, Posts, Smiths, and others, who were subsequently the settlers of Norwich and vicinity.*

These were among the men of sterling excellence of character, who assisted in laying the foundations of Connecticut, and who devoted their eminent abilities, their time, and their estates, to the great purposes of civil and religious freedom. With such men it was the privilege and the happiness of Mr. Hooker to be associated more or less, during the last eleven years of his life and labors for Connecticut and for New England at large. To have associated and acted with such men, and by the exercise of his wisdom and influence in their councils, in relation to the affairs of the rising Commonwealth, to have contributed so richly to make Connecticut what it was in its youth, and what it has since been, was honor not inferior to that of any other man whose name is registered in the history of New England.

The learned and venerable President Dwight, whose long residence in Connecticut led him to

* Trumbull's Hist. Conn., I.

study its history with much care, thus writes of Mr. Hooker :

" On the affairs of the infant colony, his influence was commanding. Little was done without his approbation ; and almost every thing which he approved was done of course. The measures which were actually adopted under his influence were contrived and executed with so much felicity, as to have sustained, with high reputation, the scrutiny of succeeding ages. Happily he infused his spirit not only into his cotemporaries, but into most of those who in succeeding generations have been entrusted with the public interests of this State. A distinguished share of the moderation, wisdom and firmness, which adorned Mr. Hooker, has been conspicuous in the public measures of Connecticut down to the present day.* An equal degree of uniformity in public measures, has not, so far as I know, existed in any country for the same length of time. Certainly there has been no such continued uniformity of wisdom and moderation ; of measures which rarely demanded to be retraced ; on which party spirit had so little influence ; or in which passion or prejudice was so little conspicuous. For this charac-

* Written in 1810.

ter the inhabitants of Connecticut are eminently indebted to the great and good man who is the subject of these remarks. If I may be allowed to give an opinion, he was the wisest of all those distinguished colonists who had a peculiar influence on the early concerns of this country." *

But it was not alone in the promotion of the fundamental interests of Connecticut, that Mr. Hooker labored for the last eleven years of his life. He had lived nearly three years, as we have already seen, in the colony of Massachusetts Bay; and had been associated with Governor Winthrop, senior, and with Cotton, Norton, and many other good men of that colony, in planning and carrying into execution, measures civil and religious, which were fundamental in all the subsequent interests of Massachusetts. Strong points of resemblance in the characteristics of Connecticut and Massachusetts have been obvious, from the first. To account for these resemblances is easy, when we consider the fact, that in the separate catalogues of their wise, great and good men are recorded some of the same names,—and among the first class of them, the name of Thomas Hooker,—men in

* Dwight's Travels, vol. I., pp. 238, 239.

Connecticut who came from the highest ranks of influence, office and usefulness in Massachusetts, to do for Connecticut what they had done for that State. With all becoming courtesy and respect, but with entire New England frankness, may it be said, therefore, Massachusetts is under high obligations to Hooker and his associates,—as instruments in the hands of a merciful Providence,—for what she too has been and still is, as an honorable member of the Union.

But it is proper to go farther still. The name NEW ENGLAND, is a name which is loved and cherished by more than four millions of people, who fill its cities, towns and villages; and who spread themselves abroad upon its plains, and over its hills, and among its valleys and mountains, and along its rivers. It is also loved and cherished by still other millions, who call New England their native country, or trace to its families their parentage and ancestry; and who, from the west, and the south, look to New England and call it the home of their own childhood, or the home of their fathers. It is due to the name and memory of Thomas Hooker, that the fact be stated, as pertaining to the present memoir, that in the original plan for the confederation, called by the name of "the United Colonies of New England," he was from the first, actively, and earnestly concerned.

Governor Winthrop, in his journal under date of 1639, has the following passage: "Mr. Haynes, the Governor of Connecticut, and Mr. Hooker, &c., came into the bay and staid near a month. It appeared by them, that they were desirous to secure the treaty of confederation with us, and though themselves would not move it, yet, by their means, it was moved by our General Court, and adopted; for they were in some doubt of the Dutch, who had lately received a new Governor, a more discreet and sober man than the former, and one who did complain much of the injury done to them at Connecticut, and very forward to hold correspondence with us, and was very inquisitive how things stood between us and them of Connecticut, which occasioned us the more readily to renew the former treaty, that the Dutch might not take notice of any breach or alienation between us."*

The transaction thus recorded was doubtless preparatory to that which Winthrop records "Mo. 3, 10," 1643, as follows:

"At this Court came the Commissioners from

---

* Savage's Winthrop, I, 299.

Plymouth, Connecticut and New Haven, viz., from Plymouth, Mr. Edward Winslow and Mr. Collier; from Connecticut, Mr. Haynes and Mr. Hopkins, with whom Mr. Fenwick of Saybrook joined; from New Haven, Mr. Theophilus Eaton and Mr. Grigson. Our Court chose a Committee to treat with them, viz., the Governor and Mr. Dudley and Mr. Bradstreet, being of the magistrates, and of the deputies Captain Gibbons, Mr. Tyng the treasurer and Mr. Hathorn. These coming to a consultation encountered some difficulties, but being all desirous of union and studious of peace, they readily yielded to each other in such things as tended to common utility, &c., so as in some two or three meetings they lovingly accorded upon these ensuing articles, which being allowed by our Court, and signed by all the Commissioners, were sent to be also ratified by the General Courts of other jurisdictions; only Plymouth Commissioners, having power only to treat, but not to determine, deferred the signing of them till they came home, but soon after they were ratified by their General Court also."*

The preamble to the articles of confederation will best answer the inquiry what were the ob-

* Savage's Winthrop, I, 99, 100.

jects of its establishment; and is in the terms following:

"Whereas we all came into these parts of America with one and the same end, namely, to advance the kingdom of our Lord Jesus Christ, and to enjoy the liberties of the gospel in purity, with peace; and whereas by our settling, by the wise providence of God, we are further dispersed upon the sea-coasts and rivers than was at first intended, so that we cannot according to our desire, with convenience communicate in one government and jurisdiction; and whereas we live encompassed with people of several nations and strange languages, which hereafter may prove injurious to us or our posterity; and forasmuch as the natives have formerly committed sundry insolencies and outrages upon several plantations of the English, and have of late combined themselves against us, and seeing by reason of the sad distractions in England, (which they have heard of) and by which they know we are hindered both from that humble way of seeking advice, and reaping those comfortable fruits of protection, which at other times we might well expect; we therefore do conceive it our bounden duty, without delay, to enter into a present consociation among ourselves for mutual help and strength in all future concernment, that, as in nation and religion, so in other respects, we be and continue one, according to the tenor and true meaning of the ensuing articles:

"Wherefore it is fully agreed and concluded between the parties above named, and they jointly and severally do, by these presents, agree and conclude that they all be, and henceforth be called by the name of the United Colonies of New England."

The articles of confederation were twelve; and were so framed as to answer, in the best manner, the objects of it, as set forth in the preamble above quoted."*

"And" (we quote from Hon. John Quincy Adams) "the New England confederacy of 1643 was the model and prototype of the North American confederacy of 1774." "New England, as a community, has by her incorporation in the North American Union, lost her distinctive character; and to the superficial observer, little remains of her but the name. As a portion of the great community of the North American Union, the unity and simplicity of her charac-

* For a more particular account of these Articles, the reader is referred to Hon. John Quincy Adams' discourse, at the second centennial anniversary of the event, May, 1843, as given in Mass. Hist. Coll., XXIX, 189—223. Also for the Articles themselves, see Savage's Winthrop, II, 101—106.

ter, without being totally extinguished, have been transformed into one component part of a stupendous republican empire, — an empire already bounded only by the Atlantic and Pacific oceans, and, to the eye of prophetic inspiration, to be hereafter bounded only by the eternal ice of the northern and southern pole."

"We have been told that it was a day-dream of our Puritan forefathers, the first settlers of New England, that they were destined to be the founders of such an empire. The foundation upon which *they* held this edifice was to be erected was the natural equality of mankind, and the two eternal pillars upon which it was to stand were *civil and religious liberty.* The natural equality of mankind, a doctrine which they imbibed from the sacred fountain of the Scriptures, taught in the history of the creation, and forming the foundation of the religion of Jesus, settled it forever, that this empire must be that kingdom of Christ against which the gates of hell shall not prevail. For this foundation, the natural equality of mankind,—and for these two pillars, civil and religious liberty,—the North American Union, to whatever extent of dominion and whatever succession of ages destined to endure, will be forever indebted to the Puritan Fathers of New England."

Mr. Hooker does not appear as a member of the board of Commissioners who completed the confederacy. Very properly it was composed of civilians only. Nor was it necessary that he should be a member, to prove his concern in it. There are some men,—and he seems to have been such an one,—who, when a great public object, which they may have been concerned in originating, is ready for its completion, are satisfied to retire and be no farther known in the transaction. To such a man as Hooker it was probably no sacrifice to stand aside, and let others enjoy the honor of publicly and officially executing the plan upon which his heart had been set,—it would seem,—from the day he began his work at Hartford. Whether his concern in it was then known beyond the breasts of Haynes and Winthrop, and the other civil fathers of the colonies who with him had been considering it; and whether posterity would ever discover his individual concern in it, probably were not questions with which he troubled himself a moment. While his friends, Haynes, Hopkins, Winslow, Collier, Fenwick, Eaton, Grigson, Dudley, Bradstreet, Gibbons, Tyng and Hathorn, were in Boston, finishing the work he had assisted in commencing, and for which he had sought the blessing of "the Father of lights;" and were really forming "the model and prototype of the North American Confederacy of 1774;" Hooker was probably in his little study, in the retired parsonage in Hartford; perhaps framing, from his Bible, that "Survey of the Summe of Church Discipline," in which are embodied some of the choicest elements of the Ecclesiastical polity in which the Congregational Churches of New England have so long prospered and rejoiced; or perhaps he was writing sermons; perhaps composing that choice little book, "The Poor Doubting Christian Drawn to Christ," or his "Soul's Preparation for Christ;" or his Commentary on the Intercessory Prayer of Christ. Great as had been the subjects involved in the well-being of the State, on which he had employed his thoughts, and which were at that moment occupying the civil fathers of the colonies in Boston; yet himself was occupied with the higher themes of the gospel he so loved to preach, and seeking to build up in the hearts of men that "kingdom of God" which is "righteousness and peace and joy in the Holy Ghost."

The eleven short and swift years of Mr. Hooker's life in Connecticut, in the history of the State were marked with the rapid maturity and execution of wise and great plans for the public good. The period was also distinguished with the signal prosperity of almost every interest contemplated by the good men of the State and the time; this, too, under many and great embarrassments. Not the least of these embarrassments was, the liability in which the colonies of the State lived, of being embroiled in wars with the Indian tribes around them, and the actual state of war in which they sometimes were. It became necessary that the militia of Connecticut should be in good organization for the purposes of defence, on any emergency; and for this end, to place at its head an efficient commanding officer. This office was assigned to Captain John Mason, as Major General. On the occasion of his being invested with this office, Mr. Hooker was designated as the person to deliver to him publicly, the military staff, with an accompanying address.* Prince, in his introduction to Mason's History of the memorable capture of the Pequot fort, at Mistick, said, of Mr. Hooker's delivery of the staff to General Mason, "We may imagine he did it with that superior piety, spirit and majesty, which were peculiar to him; like an ancient prophet, addressing himself to the military officer, and

* Trumbull's Hist. Conn., I, 95.

delivering to him the principal ensign of martial power, to lead the armies and fight the battles of the Lord and his people."*

The associates and cotemporaries of Mr. Hooker in the civil affairs of the colonies have been mentioned; and some of the principal events and features of their history and condition. We come now to speak of the ministers associated or cotemporary with him, and of the course of ministerial and ecclesiastical affairs, during the same period, and during Mr. Hooker's life.

The first ministers of the churches, in the colonies embraced in what is now Connecticut, were as follows. In Hartford, Mr. Hooker and Mr. Stone; in Windsor, Mr. Warham and Mr. Hewet; in Wethersfield, Mr. Prudden, (afterwards of Milford;) Saybrook Fort, Mr John Higginson; New Haven, Mr. Davenport and Mr. Samuel Eaton,—and on Mr. Eaton's removal, Mr. William Hooke; Guilford, Mr. Henry Whitfield; Wethersfield,—after the removal of Mr. Prudden to Milford,—Mr. Henry Smith; Saybrook,—after the removal of Mr. Higginson,—Mr. Thomas Peters; Fairfield, Mr. Jones; Stratford, Mr. Blackman; Stamford, Mr. Den-

* Mass. Hist. Coll., XVIII, 124.

ton; Branford, Mr. Abraham Pierson; New London, Mr. Blinman. "From these reverend fathers," says Trumbull, "the ministers of Connecticut trace their ordinations; especially from Mr. Hooker, Mr. Warham, Mr. Davenport and Mr. Stone. Some or other of these assisted in gathering the churches, and ordaining the ministers settled in their day."*

Mr. Hooker, Mr. Davenport and Mr. Stone, were accounted among the first men of these colonies, as respects piety, ministerial gifts and learning. The religious habits of the ministers of that period, as described by the venerable historian of the State already quoted, were, that "they were mighty and abundant in prayer. They not only fasted and prayed frequently with their people in public, but kept many days of secret fasting, prayer, and self-examination, in their studies. Some of them, it seems, fasted and prayed in this private manner, every week. Besides the exercises on the Lord's day, they preached lectures, not only in public, but from house to house. They were diligent and laborious in catechising and instructing the children and young people, both in public and private." †

---

* Hist. Conn., I, 279, 280.

† Trumbull's Hist. Conn., I, 280.

Whether Mr. Hooker was engaged in the theological instruction of candidates for the christian ministry, does not appear in any of the histories. From the fact, however, that the ministers of Connecticut were the principal instructors of such as were preparing for a collegiate course, and that there were no public theological schools at that period, it is beyond doubt that Mr. Hooker bore his part with his brethren, in the work of professional education of ministers. Mr. James Fitch, who in 1646, became pastor of a church organized at Saybrook, was a theological student with him.

The influence of Mr. Hooker's habits in maintaining a high standard of family religion; and in relation to which, the testimony of John Eliot has already been given,—doubtless had concern in promoting like habits in the families of other ministers in the State, as noticed by the historian of Connecticut in the following passages.

"They paid constant attention to the religion of their families. They read the Scriptures and prayed in them daily, morning and evening, and instructed all their domestics constantly to attend the secret as well as private and public duties of religion. They were attentive to the religious state of all the families and individuals of their respective flocks. As they had 'taken up the cross,' forsaken their pleasant seats and enjoyments in their native country, and followed their Saviour into 'a land not sown,' for the sake of his holy religion and the advancement of his kingdom; they sacrificed all worldly interests to these glorious purposes." *

Connecticut has been proverbial in former years, as "the land of steady habits." And men who hate serious religion, have often made these habits the subject of ridicule. But even these have thus given indirect testimony to the worth of such habits. It is not presuming too much, nor boasting improperly of the power of ministerial influence, to express the opinion, that Connecticut has been "the land of steady habits," because the ministers, like Hooker, Davenport and others, were men who "commanded their children and their households after them, to keep the ways of the Lord." Genuine Puritanism begins its work, for the good of the Church and the State in the family; and sends out its salutary influences into society, from as many fountains as there are families in which it presides. Amidst such influences immorality cannot live, in the forms of profaneness, intemperance, sabbath-breaking, impurity, disobedi-

* Trumbull, I, 281, 282.

ence to parents, fraud, injustice. This was a striking feature in the times of Hooker and his worthy brethren in the Connecticut ministry.*

With such ministers, the churches highly esteemed the preaching of the gospel and the ordinances of the New Testament. The churches of that time were small, so that except in the largest, there were not more than sixteen or eighteen male members ; and in some not more than eight or nine. Yet, they were determined to support the gospel. Neither poverty, nor dangers from the savage tribes around them, nor any inconveniences or privations incident to their residence in a wilderness, could prevent their maintenance of the gospel ministry. It was their solace and comfort under the trials of this life. It showed them their glorious hope for the life to come. With ministers of such devout and heavenly spirit, and of such sanctified wisdom as appeared in Hooker and his brethren of the sacred office, "the wilderness and the solitary places were glad," and "the desert" did "rejoice and blossom as the rose."

In the notices already recorded, of Mr. Hooker's ministry while he resided in England, it has appeared, that he earnestly promoted the

* Trumbull, I, 282.

intercourse of ministers with each other, for their mutual benefit and advancement in fitness for their work. His love for the society of his brethren, carried with him, wherever he went, and living and active in him wherever he fixed his home, was probably concerned in the establishment of those ministerial organizations in Connecticut, which exist at this day. " Stated meetings of ministers, which may be traced back to the earliest days of the churches, (says the author of Ratio Disciplinæ,*) were approved and recommended particularly by the venerable Hooker. It is affirmed, that during the whole of his ministerial life, the pastors in the neighborhood of his residence held frequent meetings for the purpose of mutual consultation and advice in religious things. One of the last and emphatic sayings of this father of the churches, was, '*we must agree upon constant meetings of ministers.*' " It was remarked of him while residing in Essex, England, " The godly ministers round about the country would have recourse to him, to be directed and resolved in their difficult cases; and it was by his means that these godly ministers held their monthly

* pp. 149, 150.

meetings for fasting, prayer and profitable conferences."

Here is one of the grand secrets of that ever living harmony and fraternal love, and union of views and aims and influence, which, for more than two hundred years has been the beauty and strength of the Congregational ministry in New England. The ministerial bodies take different forms and names, in the different States. In Connecticut, the ancient home of Thomas Hooker, and the scene of his most happy influence, they appear in three different organizations.* First, the Monthly Minister's Meeting, which embraces a small number, conveniently situated for assembling with that measure of frequency. Secondly, the Association, which embraces the ministers of a county, when not too large in extent; and meeting annually or semi-annually. Thirdly, the General Association of the State; in which the county or district associations meet by delegation, annually; and upon the sessions of which, delegates from foreign bodies attend. Mr. Hooker, and the other ministers of Connecticut, and those of Massachusetts, probably, all held the same general views on the subject

* See "Congregational Order," published by direction of Gen. Asso. Conn., 1845.

of ministerial intercourse in associations of this description; and laid, unitedly, the foundations of our present New England ministerial associations. They are eminently Puritan organizations. They have been the model for similar associations in New York and the West, which feel the influence of New England. And blessed be the memory of every Puritan father of this land who assisted in thus devising good for the Congregational ministry and Churches of our country, for generations past, present, and to come.

Let it here be distinctly understood, that the honor of organizing Congregational Associations is not claimed exclusively for Thomas Hooker. It had a higher than human origin, in the gracious promptings of that "One Spirit," who shed abroad "love to the brethren" in his heart and the hearts of his cotemporary laborers in the ministry. "He, the Spirit of Truth," has thus bound his servants together, in circles smaller or larger; and has made the Congregational ministry, who hold the truth, to be one body; animated by the same spirit, and devoting themselves to the one great object, dear to "faithful men," "the edifying of the body of Christ."

Mr. Hooker's interest, however, in Christian

associations did not stop with the ministry. He desired to see, and to promote, what in Connecticut and elsewhere is called the *Consociation* of the Churches, for the purposes of christian intercourse, and mutual aid in affairs ecclesiastical. These bodies, called Consociations, in Connecticut, have always been composed of pastors and delegates of the churches. The largest proportion of the churches of Connecticut proper, are, and have been, from the early years of its settlement, it is believed, organized in Consociations. The author of Magnalia Americana remarks of Mr. Hooker, "he was an hearty friend unto the *Consociation of Churches*," and speaks of frequent meetings held during his life, in which, it is supposed, the churches were represented.*

It would seem, indeed, that nothing could be more natural, than that men, who had suffered, as he and his brethren of the ministry and of the churches had suffered, in England, from the oppressions of the bishops, should here seek the advantages and the comforts of both ministerial and ecclesiastical parity. Driven hither for liberty, civil and ecclesiastical, and to their Bibles for instruction on the forms both of min-

* Mather, I, 316.

isterial and ecclesiastical association, accordant with the liberty of the gospel, they came to practical conclusions, which could not fail, with the divine blessing, to ensure their highest prosperity and happiness.

The general views of ecclesiastical order and discipline which Mr. Hooker entertained, and promoted among the churches of the Connecticut colonies, were substantially those which shortly before the close of his life, he embodied in his admirable work, " A Survey of the Summe of Church Discipline." Of this work, a particular account will be given in a subsequent chapter. It will be sufficient here, to remark, that in regard to the officers of the church, and the source of their authority, his views were strictly Congregational. In other words, Hooker was an *ecclesiastical republican.* In common parlance, and in distinction from the term Episcopal, the churches of Connecticut are sometimes called *Presbyterian.* But in point of fact there never were Presbyterian churches in Connecticut, till, within a very few years, they have been organized from Scotch population settled in a very few manufacturing villages. Mr. Hooker's work, to which allusion has just been made, was indeed written, in part, for the purpose of controverting the main positions of

Presbyterianism, as at that time set forth by writers in Scotland and England; and to draw the lines of demarcation between Congregationalism and Presbyterianism, as two very different systems of church government. And that effort was successful. The influence of his book on the ecclesiastical polity of the Congregational churches of Connecticut was decisive and permanent. Connecticut Congregationalism, in all its essential elements, will be found in Hooker's "Survey of the Summe of Church Discipline."

Between this system of ecclesiastical polity, as being essentially republican, and the civil constitution of Connecticut, there has ever been good agreement. The men who there sought religious liberty, and formed the Churches upon the broad basis of that freedom which belongs to christian men, really laid the foundation of the civil State when they laid those of the Churches.* Christian men in the Congregational denomination in Connecticut, therefore,—and the same is true throughout New England and in our Western Churches, of the same order,—are never perplexed by having to act upon one system in the Church, and upon

* Trumbull's Hist. I, 282.

another in civil society. They are perfectly at home in both spheres of action. Every Congregational Christian's rights and privileges and duties are the same, properly considered, in the one as in the other. And where Congregational polity has prevalence, there need be no fear of a "union between Church and State."

That which Mr. Hooker did to promote a scriptural and just ecclesiastical polity, he did also to promote a sound and orthodox faith. His published writings,—though but in small proportion theological, in the technical use of the term,—were thoroughly after the Puritan model, as to doctrines. The history of the Confessions of Faith, adopted by the Congregational Churches of Connecticut, gives evidence that the same individual instrumentality which had been concerned in modeling their polity, was also employed in settling their articles of religious belief. If, in more recent times, changes have been made, in the articles of any Churches in New England, by the substitution of feeble, unmeaning, or doubtful generalities, in order to satisfy minds reluctant to receive a plain-spoken New Testament orthodoxy; still, a good proportion of the Churches, it is believed, have adhered to the Puritan faith, by preserving inviolate the "form of doctrine" drawn from the "sure word," and received and preached by such men as Thomas Hooker.

This "soundness in the faith" prepared Mr. Hooker and his brethren in the New England colonies, to protest, fearlessly and faithfully, against heresy, in any and every form. When therefore Antinomianism found its way into Massachusetts, Hooker and Davenport as representatives from the Churches in the Colonies of Connecticut and New Haven, in the first general council in New England, bore their testimony against error, with the intrepidity and fidelity which became lovers of "the truth of Christ."*

Thus did this father in the early Churches of Connecticut, assist in laying deep and broad the foundations of ecclesiastical order, of a pure faith, of spiritual prosperity, and of a healthful, moral and civil condition in the Commonwealth.

Mr. Hooker's influence and usefulness, however, were not confined within the bounds of the Connecticut Colonies. He appears to have been regarded as the common property of the Churches in all the New England Colonies at that period. He was frequently present in the ecclesiastical assemblies of the confederacy, as

* Trumbull's Hist. Conn, I, 288, 289.

well as in those of his own colony and of others in his immediate vicinity. He was relied upon for aid in the promotion of all the great objects which were undertaken for the common weal of the Churches; especially where difficulties were to be adjusted, and a wise and safe direction was to be given to the religious action of the Churches and the ministry. He was one of the Moderators of the first New England Synod, held at Cambridge, for the examination of certain erroneous opinions which had been set forth by Mr. Wheelwright and Mrs. Hutchinson, to the disturbance of the peace of the Churches in Massachusetts Bay. Accompanied by other ministers from the colonies of Connecticut, he come to Boston several days previous to the assembling of the Synod, and as the result of consultation, with the consent of the magistrates, a day was appointed to be kept by all the Churches as a day of humiliation.* He was also active during that time, in endeavors to bring about a reconciliation between Mr. Cotton, Mr. Wheelwright and Mr. Wilson; in reference, apparently, to some personal matters. And here is a fact which affords additional presump-

* Savage's Winthrop, I, 235—241; Mass. Hist. Coll., IX, 32; XV, 298.

tive evidence against Robertson's imputation upon Hooker's motives in removing to Connecticut, and noticed in a previous chapter. If Cotton and Hooker could not live together in Massachusetts, on account of unfriendly rivalship and jealousy, it does not seem very probable that Hooker would have been called from Connecticut to officiate as a peace-maker between Cotton and his neighbors.

The respect of a large number of great and good men, in England, for Mr. Hooker, and their confidence in his soundness in faith and in his fidelity to the cause of truth and liberty on both sides of the Atlantic, were indicated by the invitation which he received,—together with Mr. Cotton and Mr. Davenport,—to be a member of that memorable body, the Westminster Assembly of Divines, which was convened in London in the year 1642. This passage in the history of the calling of an Assembly which gave to the Christian world those admirable digests of religious faith and practice, *the Larger and Shorter Westminster Catechism,* will doubtless interest the reader; not only as affording proof of the regard in which Hooker, Cotton and Davenport were held, in England; but also as indicating who were the prominent men in calling that assembly of divines.*

The reception of these invitations to the Westminster Assembly, occasioned a meeting of the magistrates and ministers of Massachusetts, who were nearest Boston, for consultation and advice. "Most of them," remarks Hutchinson, "were of opinion that it was a call of God. Mr. Davenport was inclined to go; but his church were unwilling to release him, he being at that time their only minister. Mr. Cotton thought it a clear call, and would have undertaken the voyage, if the others would have gone with him. Mr. Hooker did not like the business, and thought it not a sufficient call, to go a thousand leagues to confer about matters of church government."

It seems that the communications received from England on this subject, did not give intimations of the objects of the convocation sufficiently definite; and left upon the mind of Mr. Hooker, particularly, the impression, that "matters of church government" were to be the principal, if not the only subject of consideration. Aware of the probability that the Presbyterian preferences of the English members of the

* For the copy of the document accompanying the letters of invitation to the three men, see Appendix B.

Assembly would prevail, he doubtless preferred not to come into collision with his brethren there, upon that subject; fearing that his brethren of New England and himself would stand alone as the advocates of Congregationalism. Having advocated, intelligently and conscientiously, the principles of pure Congregationalism ever since he came to New England; and being at this time, doubtless, engaged in maturing his "Survey of the Summe of Church Discipline," as the result of prayerful and deliberate study of the Scriptures, it was quite natural that he should feel reluctant to cross the Atlantic and go directly into a controversy with his English brethren on the subject of Church Polity, without any hope of changing the opinions of the Presbyterian members of the Assembly, and being quite certain that he should not change his own for theirs. His refusal to accept the invitation to himself, therefore, is not to be regarded as by any means unfraternal in itself; but as a measure in which he was acting upon the wise man's advice, to "leave off contention before it be meddled with;" and in which, also, he should keep himself unembarrassed in his future advocacy of Congregationalism at home.

Apart from these reasons, and with our eyes upon that admirable digest of faith and practice, the Westminster Catechism, drawn up by that Assembly, and which every Orthodox Congregationalist as well as Presbyterian, in America, approves and loves at this day, we wish it could be said by us, that in framing that instrument, three such men as Hooker, Cotton, and Davenport, from New England, had borne a part. As it is, however, we rejoice that the Westminster Catechism constitutes such a bond of faith and affection as it surely does, between the Congregational and the Presbyterian churches of America. This fact testifies to the world that there are two distinct christian denominations in it, who, while they differ in their church polity, are "one and indivisible" with respect to their faith in "the gospel of God our Saviour."

That Mr. Hooker shared largely, with his brethren of the New England ministry, in the regard of the churches, is indicated by the evidence of affection, veneration, and delight in his preaching, which his visits to Massachusetts always elicited. Whenever *the old pastor of Newtown* was to preach in that vicinity, the gathering of a crowded and attentive assembly was quite certain. He was one of those "ministers of Christ" towards whom the feelings of the true people of God literally fulfilled that apostolic injunction, "to esteem them very highly in love, for their work's sake." Nor is there any affection felt in human hearts, on this side of heaven, which is warmer, holier, or more elevated than that which is borne by true Christians towards the "good and faithful servant" of the Lord Jesus, by whom they have been fed with the good and precious word of divine grace; the pious and eloquent preacher who has

> "Allured to brighter worlds, and led the way."

But "the time drew near that Israel must die." The devoted and heavenly-minded christian, the "able minister of the New Testament," the planter of churches, the founder of a state, the guardian of the liberties of both the church and the state, the "ambassador for Christ," who had "borne, and had patience, and for Christ's name's sake had labored and had not fainted;" he who had been so rich a blessing to the children of God in "the father land," and to the infant churches of New England, was about to be called home to his rest and his reward. Not that he had become too old to labor longer in the service of Christ, for he was yet many years short of "three-score and ten;" nor that he was prematurely worn out, for we find no intimation that his health, subsequent to his residence in Holland, was ever impaired. The messenger of death finally appeared in a violent epidemic disease, which in a brief space accomplished its work upon the strong man in the midst of his days.

Of this epidemic, and of the death of Mr. Hooker as one of its victims, Governor Winthrop makes the following record:

"An epidemical sickness was through the country, among Indians and English, French and Dutch. It took them like a cold, and a light fever with it. Such as bled or used cooling drinks died; those who took comfortable things, for most part recovered, and that in few days. Wherein a special providence of God appeared, for not a family, nor but few persons escaping it; had it brought all so weak as it did some, and continued so long, our hay and corn had been lost for want of help; but such was the mercy of God to his people, as few died, not above forty or fifty in Massachusetts, and near as many at Connecticut. But that which made the stroke more sensible and grievous, both to them and to all the country, was the death of that faithful servant of the Lord, Mr. Thomas Hooker, pastor of the church in Hartford, who, for piety, prudence, wisdom, zeal, learning, and what else might make him serviceable in the place and time he lived in, might be compared with men of greatest note; and he shall need no other praise; the fruits of his labors in both Englands shall preserve an honorable and happy remembrance of him forever."*

Mr. Hooker had been known to some of his friends to say, "that he should esteem it a favor from God, if he might live no longer than he should be able to hold up lively in the work of his place; and that when the time of his departure should come, God would shorten the time." His wish was granted. It appeared that his passage from his pulpit to his grave and to heaven, was, in divine mercy, appointed to be short. The history of his last days will be best given in the language of one who seems to have delighted to record the histories of the good men of "the former times," and of their triumphant departures "to be with Christ."†

"Some of his most observant hearers noticed an astonishing cloud in his congregation, the last Lord's day of his public ministry, when he administered the Lord's supper among them; and a most unaccountable heaviness and sleepiness, even of the most watchful christians of the place; not unlike the drowsiness of the disci-

* Winthrop's Hist. of New Eng., II, 310.

† See Mather's Magnalia.

ples, when our Lord was going to die; for which one of the elders publicly rebuked them. When those devout people afterwards perceived that this was the last sermon and sacrament, wherein they were to have the presence of their pastor with them; 'tis inexpressible, how much they bewailed their inattentiveness to his farewell dispensations; and some of them could enjoy no peace in their own souls, until they had obtained leave of the elders to confess, before the whole congregation, with many tears, that inadvertency.

"In the time of his sickness he did not say much to the standers by; but being asked that he would utter his apprehensions about some important things, especially about the state of New England, he answered, 'I have not that work now to do; I have already declared the counsel of the Lord.' And when one that stood weeping by his bed-side, said to him, 'Sir, you are going to receive the reward of all your labors,' he replied, '*Brother, I am going to receive mercy.*' At last he closed his eyes with his own hands, and gently stroking his own forehead, with a smile in his countenance, he gave a little groan, and so expired his blessed soul into the arms of his fellow servants, the holy angels, on July 7, 1647. In which last hours, the glorious peace of soul which he had enjoyed without any interruption for near thirty years together, so gloriously accompanied him, that a worthy spectator, writing to Mr. Cotton a relation thereof, made this reflection: 'Truly, sir, the sight of his death will make me have more pleasant thoughts of death than ever I yet had in my life.'"

His beloved associate in the ministry of the church at Hartford writes, under date July 19, 1647, to Mr. Thomas Shepard, pastor of the church at Cambridge:—

"Dearest Brother:

"God brought us safely to Hartford; but when I came hither God presented to me a sad spectacle. Mr. Hooker looked like a dying man. God refused to hear our prayers for him, but tooke him from us, July 7, a little before sunne-set. Our sun is set, our light is eclipsed, our joy is darkened. We remember now in the dayes of our calamitie, the pleasant things we enjoyed in former times. His spirits and head were so oppressed with the disease, that he was not able to expresse much to us in his sicknesse; but had expressed to Mr. Goodwin before my returne, that his peace was made in heaven, and had continued 30 years without alteration. He was above Satan. 'Marke the upright man, for the end of that man is peace!' He lived a most blamelesse life. I think his greatest enemies cannot charge him. He hath done much work for Christ, and now rests from his labours, and his workes follow him. But our loss is great, and bitter. My losse is bitter. I gave thankes to my God daily for his helpe; and no man in the world but myself, knowes what a friend he hath been unto me. As his abilities were great, so his love and faithfulnesse were very great. I can never look to have the like fellow officer in his place. There are but few such men in the world. I will say no more, least I should seeme to exceed. It is an extream difficultie to me to know how to behave myself under the hand of God which strikes me in a speciall manner. Praye for me in this stresse: for I am astonished at this amazing providence. I cannot complain of God, who 'doeth all things well.' The Lord shew me what his mind is, that I may be rightly affected with this losse. I pray suggest, what you thinke may be the mind of God in it.

"Mrs. Hooker was taken with the same sickness, that night when I came to Hartford, and was very neer death. She is yet weake, but I hope recovering. It would have been a great aggravation of our miserie if God had blotted out that pleasant familie all at once."—"My wife is sick and weake; I am not well, I am troubled with heat and faintnesse. The last night I had some rest, but the night before I could not sleep all the night, but slumber and dreame. God gives me warning to prepare for my change. The glorious presence of Christ in heaven is much better than life. We wait for that blessed hope. If it had not been for this occasion, I know not whether I should have written any thing at this time, being unfit to write. We shall doe what we can to prepare Mr. Hooker's answer to Rutherford,* that it may be sent before winter."

fr: t: Sam: Stone."

Superscribed: "To his dear Brother,
Mr. Thomas Shepard, Pastor of the church at Cambridge."

When Mr. Hooker was departed, it was felt, throughout New England, that a strong and majestic pillar had been removed from the church and from the state. But not less was it felt, also, that a public benefactor, and a "good and faithful servant" of God had taken his up-

* Survey of Church Discipline.

ward flight, to enter into the rest and holiness and bliss of heaven, and to receive, at the hands of "the Lord the righteous Judge," a "crown of righteousness."

His age was 61 years. His death took place on the anniversary of his birth. He died "in his full strength," not having reached the period when infirmities impair usefulness, and years weigh down the man into the tomb. Thus it often is, in the providence of God, that the men who appear in the midst of life and usefulness, and whose continuance seems most desirable, are taken away as in a moment, and the churches are left in tears.

## CHAPTER VI.

Estimate of Mr. Hooker's character in various points. Rank in the esteem of his brethren in the ministry. Prayerfulness. Humility, and its exemplifications. Disinterestedness. Solicitude on the dangers of the churches. Natural temper and spirit. Self-control. Treatment of errors, and of those with whom he was necessarily in controversy. Intercourse with his brethren of the ministry. Kind interest in young ministers. Generosity to the necessitous. Character as a pastor and administrator of church government. Admission of members to the church. Social character and intercourse.

In considering the character of Mr. Hooker, as separate from the history of his life, and in a more general view, it will be proper that we look at the estimation in which he was held, and the rank assigned him by his brethren in the christian ministry, and by those whom he served in the office of pastor and spiritual guide. He appears to have been a man, with respect to whose great excellence and eminence, in various important points of character, the great and good men of his own time united in bearing testimony.

The author of Magnalia Americana thus

gives the testimony of several, principally his cotemporaries: "Mr. Henry Whitfield, having spent many years in studying of books, did at length take two or three years to study men; and in pursuance of this design, having acquainted himself with the most considerable divines of England, at last fell into the acquaintance of Mr. Hooker; concerning whom he afterwards gave this testimony, 'that he had not thought there had been such a man on earth; a man in whom there shone so many excellencies as were in this incomparable Hooker; a man in whom learning and wisdom were so tempered with zeal, holiness, and watchfulness.' "

His pupil, Mr. Ash, gave this opinion concerning him: "For his great abilities and glorious services, both in this and the other England, he deserves a place in the first rank of those whose lives are of late recorded." Mr. Ezekiel Rogers, another of his cotemporaries, spoke of him as a "rich pearl," possessed by America. Mr. Elisha Corlet, of Cambridge, England, who was an early teacher of many of the worthy men that came to this country for the sake of "faith and a good conscience," celebrated his virtues in a Latin elegy, breathing alike the friendship of the refined scholar, and the affectionate admiration of the christian brother. Increase Mather, in his preface to the lives of Cotton, Norton, Wilson, Davenport, and Hooker, remarks of the latter, in his quaint style, "Great pity it is, that no more can be collected of the memorables relating to so good and so great a man as he was; than whom Connecticut never did, and perhaps never will see a greater person." "It was a black day to New England when that great light was removed." With the learned and able Dr. William Ames, the well known author of "Medulla Theologiæ," Mr. Hooker had in Holland spent some time, and had assisted him in the preparation of his work, entitled "A fresh suit against ceremonies."—"Such was the regard which Dr. Ames had for him, that notwithstanding his own vast ability and experience, yet when it came to the narrow of any question about the instituted worship of God, he would still profess himself conquered by Mr. Hooker's reason; declaring that, though he had been acquainted with many scholars of divers nations, yet he never met with Mr. Hooker's equal, either for preaching or disputing."* Mr. Cotton, in his preface to Mr. Norton's answer to Apollonius, says of Mr. Hooker, "Dominatur in Concionibus," and in an elegy upon his death, thus writes of him:

* Mather, I, 308.

"'Twas of Geneva's worthies said, with wonder,
(Those worthies three) *Farel* was wont to thunder;
*Viret* like rain or tender grass to shower,
But *Calvin*, lively oracles to pour.
All these in Hooker's spirit did remain,
A son of thunder and a shower of rain;
A pourer forth of lively oracles;
In saving souls, the sum of miracles."

The estimation in which he was held by his church and people, is learned from passages in an epistle prefatory to his Survey of Church Discipline, published after his decease, and signed by Edward Hopkins and William Goodwin: "We have for many years lived under God's shadow, been fed with the dainties of his house, enjoyed the full improvement of the large abilities of faithful watchmen and overseers for our good, to whom our comforts and welfare in every kind have been precious. But the only wise God, for our great unworthiness, has lately made a sad breach upon us, by the death of our most dear pastor, whereby our glory is much eclipsed, our comforts not a little impaired, and our fears justly multiplied. The stroke is direful and amazing, when such a stake is taken out of the hedge, such a pillar from the house, such a pastor from his flock, in such a time and place as this.

"It is not our purpose, or is it suitable to our

condition, to lay out the breadth of the excellencies wherewith, through the abundant grace of the Lord, he was enriched and fitted for the service of his great name; or if we were willing to improve ourselves in that kind, have our pens received an anointing for such employment. What we express is only to put you and ourselves in mind of the invaluable loss we have sustained, that our hearts being deeply and duly affected under that sad afflicting providence, we may look up to the Holy One of Israel our Redeemer, who teacheth to profit that instruction may be sealed up unto us thereby.

"He was (as you well know,) one of a thousand whose diligence and unweariedness, besides his other endowments in the work committed to him, was almost beyond compare. He revealed the whole counsel of the Lord unto us, kept nothing back, dividing the word aright. His care was of strong and weak, sheep and lambs, to give a portion to each in due season; delighting in holy administrations, which by him were held forth in much beauty and glory. In this work his Master found him, and so called him to enter into his glory. Some of you are not ignorant with what strength of importunity he was drawn to the present service, and with what fear and care he attended it. The weight and difficulty of the work was duly apprehended by him, and he looked upon it as somewhat unsuitable to a pastor whose head and heart and hands were full of the employments of his proper place.

"Besides, his spirit most delighted in the search of the mystery of Christ, in the 'unsearchable riches' thereof, and the work and method of the Spirit in the communication of the same unto the soul for its everlasting welfare; some discovery whereof may hereafter be presented to the world, as the Lord gives liberty and opportunity.

"Such strength of parts clothed with humility, such clear and high apprehensions of the things of God, with a ready, cheerful condescending to the infirmities of the weak, (which was his daily study and practice,) are not often to be found among the sons of men, nor yet the sons of God in this world."

The man who took such a hold on the affections of both ministers and private christians in the ranks of the church, and to whom was awarded so high a place in their respect and confidence, must have been a minister of no ordinary worth.

Mr. Hooker's devotional habits were of an exemplary character. "He was a man of prayer which was indeed a ready way to become a man of God. He would say that 'prayer was the principal part of a minister's work; it was this by which he was to carry on the rest.'—Accordingly he still devoted one day in a month to private prayer with fasting before the Lord, besides the public fasts which often occurred unto him. He would say that such extraordinary favors as the life of religion and the power of godliness, must be preserved by the frequent use of such extraordinary means as prayer with fasting; and that if professors grow negligent of these means, iniquity will abound, and the 'love of many wax cold.' Nevertheless, in the duty of prayer he affected strength, rather than length. And though he had not so much variety in his public praying as in his public preaching, yet he always had a seasonable respect unto present occasions. And it was observed that his prayer was usually like Jacob's ladder, wherein the nearer he came to the end, the nearer he drew to heaven; and he grew into such rapturous pleadings with God and praisings of God, as made some to say that, like the master of the feast, he reserved the best wine until the last. Nor was the wonderful success of his prayers upon special concerns unobserved by the whole colony, who reckoned him the Moses who turned away the wrath of God from them, and obtained a blast from heaven upon the Indians, by his uplifted hands, in those remarkable deliverances which they sometimes experienced. It was very particularly observed when there was a battle to be fought between the Narraganset and Monhegin Indians, in the year 1643. The Narraganset Indians had complotted the ruin of the English, but the Monhegin Indians were confederated with us. And a war now being between those two nations, much notice was taken of the prevailing importunity wherewith Mr. Hooker urged for the accomplishment of that great promise unto the people of God, 'I will bless them that bless thee, and I will curse him that curseth thee.' And the effect of it was, that the Narragansets received a wonderful overthrow from the Monhegins, though the former did three or four to one exceed the latter. Such an Israel at prayer was our Hooker. And this praying pastor was blessed, as indeed such ministers use to be, with a praying people.— There fell upon his pious people a 'double portion' of the Spirit which they beheld in him."*

Such an example in pastor and people, should not be lost upon the pastors and churches of

* Magnalia, I, 312.

our own time. The question doubtless demands our serious consideration, in these days of multiplied means of religious knowledge and improvement, and of freedom from outward dangers and trials, whether there is not more dependence upon means and their use, than upon prayer for "the Spirit of grace," and upon his power, working for the holiness of the church and the regeneration of the world.

Intimately connected with prayerfulness of spirit, in the faithful minister of Christ, is humility. In this also Mr. Hooker was eminently examplary. In the time of one of his visits to his friends and former people in Massachusetts Bay, he was expected to preach; a pleasure which was naturally much desired by those who had enjoyed his ministrations before his removal to Connecticut. Perhaps there was somewhat of idolatry of affection. Mr. Hooker was to preach on May 26, 1639, Lord's day in the afternoon, at Cambridge. A great assembly was gathered, from other congregations, attracted by his fame as a preacher; among them the governor of the colony. "When he came to preach, (Winthrop says, "having gone on with much strength of voice and intention of spirit about a quarter of an hour,") he found himself so unaccountably at a loss, that after some shattered and broken attempts to proceed, he made a full stop, saying to the assembly, that 'every thing which he would have spoken was taken out of his mouth, and out of his mind also.' Wherefore he desired them to sing a psalm, while he withdrew about half an hour from them. Returning then to the congregation, he preached a most admirable sermon, wherein he held them for two hours together, in an extraordinary strain, both of pertinency and vivacity."*

Wounded pride, in a man of less grace than Mr. Hooker, would have laid to heart such an arrest of thought and of eloquence, and would have attempted explanations and palliations, or would have endeavored to account for such a mortifying failure by blaming the weather, or the confined air of a crowded assembly, or the state of his health. He took no such view of the matter. On an allusion to the divine withdrawment of assistance from him, by some of his friends, afterward, he replied, with the humility which became a preacher of the grace and duty of humility: "We daily confess that we have nothing, and can do nothing, without Christ; and what if Christ will make this mani-

* Mag. I, 311.

fest in us and on us, before our congregations? What remains but that we be humbly contented? And what manner of discouragement is there in all this?"

This is an admirable piece of instruction.—And let the minister of the gospel who ever finds himself mortified in the pulpit, by failure to execute his own conceptions of his subject and of his wishes, in preaching, and to please his hearers, wisely and humbly consider how easy it is, aye, and how necessary it may be, also, for "the Master" to strip him of pride and self; to make him ashamed, even "in the assembly of the people," that he may learn not to trust in his preparations, his powers of reasoning, rhetoric, or elocution, but to rely upon the aids of the Spirit of grace and truth.

Mr. Hooker, notwithstanding his intellectual strength and eminence, and his great reputation, "was of a very condescending spirit, not only towards his brethren in the ministry, but also towards the humblest of any christians whatsoever. He was very willing to sacrifice his own apprehensions to the convincing reason of another man, and very ready to acknowledge any mistake or failing in himself."*

* Mag., I, 313.

With such humility and habits of condescension, it is natural to look for disinterestedness. This trait of character was very prominent in Mr. Hooker. "He was born to serve many." He industriously and unceasingly sought to serve the best interests of his fellow men. It mattered not where his services were needed; whether in the duties of an instructor and preacher in Emmanuel College, at Cambridge; or of lecturer in Chelmsford; or of the more private duties of an instructor of youth at Little Baddow; or of a private counselor and helper of his brethren in the ministry, for their spiritual good, after the seal of the bishop's interdiction was upon his own lips as a preacher; or whether driven by persecution to Holland, he was assisting the labors of Paget at Amsterdam, or of Forbes at Delft, or of Ames at Rotterdam; or whether he was preaching to a company of Puritans on the middle of the Atlantic, or to a Church of pilgrims at Newtown, or to a handful of the children of God in the wilderness at Hartford. His motto seemed to be, everywhere, and at all times, "I seek not yours, but you," "yea, I will very gladly spend and be spent for you."

On the same principle he ever acted also, when called to take part in affairs of public, civil and personal interest. He was always ready to serve as a counselor, whether in endeavoring to aid in adjusting the difficulties arising out of the opinions and movements of Roger Williams; or in bringing about a reconciliation between Governor Winthrop and the deputy, Mr. Dudley; or between Cotton, Wheelwright and Wilson; or in the great work of planning the New England Confederacy; or in assisting the civil fathers of the Connecticut Colonies in their effort to furnish a sound legislation. He was a man of a large heart, and of superiority to the selfish seeking of his own advantage, as separate from the public weal, and ever prepared for self-sacrifice. He "consulted not with flesh and blood," but inquired for duty, for the true interests of the Churches, the welfare of the infant State; and beyond all, for the glory of his God and Father in heaven. A man of such a spirit needs not to be seated upon a throne, or to dwell in a palace, in order to be truly honored. He is always great in the scene of duty and usefulness; and in his influence on society, both civil and religious, he makes himself to be felt, everywhere, to good purpose.

Mr. Hooker's love to the kingdom and honor of Christ made him feel tenderly solicitous, relative to the spiritual dangers of the Churches planted in this country, in the enjoyment of so much liberty, quiet and outward prosperity. "He said that adversity had slain its thousands; but prosperity would slay its ten thousands. He feared that they who had been lively Christians in the fire of persecution, would soon become cold in the midst of universal peace; except some few, whom God, by sharp trials would keep in a faithful, watchful, humble, praying frame. But under these apprehensions, it was his own endeavor to beware of abating his own first love." "One of his predictions was, that God would punish the wanton spirit of the professors in this country, with a sad want of able men in all orders. Another was, that in certain places, of great light sinned against, there would break forth such horrible sins as would be to the amazement of the world." "In his discourses he would frequently intermix most affectionate warnings of the declensions which would quickly befall the Churches of New England."*

"He that ruleth his spirit is greater than he that taketh a city," writes the wise man. Mr. Hooker illustrated this truth, in his powerful

* Mather, I. 312, &c.

self-control. Mr. Henry Whitfield remarked of him, that "he had the best command of his own spirit, which he ever saw in any man, whatsoever. For though he was a man of a cholerick disposition, and had a mighty vigor and fervour of spirit; which as occasion served was wondrous useful to him; yet he had ordinarily as much government of his choler, as a man has of a mastiff-dog in a chain: he could let out his dog, and pull in his dog as he pleased."

When he had erred in spirit and words, under apparent provocation, he was above that smallness of soul and that disingenuousness which would descend to the meanness of denying his fault; but was ready to make the most frank acknowledgment of it to any one, however humble, whom he had injured by the expression of his feelings. An incident will illustrate this remark. Some damage had been done to one of his neighbors. Mr. Hooker, shortly after, meeting with an unlucky boy, who had the reputation of being a rogue, and believing him to be the offender, fell to chiding the boy, as the perpetrator of the mischief which had excited his indignation. "The boy denied it; and Mr. Hooker still went on in an angry manner charging him with it. Whereupon, said the boy, 'Sir, I see you are in a passion,

I'll say no more to you;' and so ran away. Mr. Hooker, upon farther inquiry, not finding that the boy could be proved guilty, sent for him. Having first, by a calm question, given the boy opportunity to renew his denial of the fact, he said to him, 'Since I cannot prove to the contrary, I am bound to believe—and I do believe—what you say;' and then added, 'Indeed I was in a passion, when I spoke to you before; it was my sin, and it is my shame, and I am truly sorry for it; and I hope in God I shall be more watchful hereafter.' So giving him some good counsel, the poor lad went away extremely affected with such a carriage in so good a man. And it proved an occasion of good to the soul of the lad all his days." *

With such habits of self-control, and with a spirit so ruled by the gospel of Christ; as might be expected, he was no angry polemic, when controversy for truth and righteousness were necessary. His pulpit was no place for angry assaults upon the errors which were abroad. Yet he stood there, always, firm and uncompromising, as a preacher of "the truth of Christ." The careful examiner of his published writings, (which in important measure

* Magnalia, I. 313.

constituted the substance of his preaching,) will find him, truly, a powerful assailant of sin and sinners of all sorts. He was a perfect "Boanerges," when it was demanded by his subject and its bearings on the consciences and conduct of men. But who needs to be taught the difference, between such preaching and that species of pulpit pugilism sometimes witnessed, in which "the old man" in the preacher, grapples with "the old man" in the hearer, from pure fondness for fighting?

We have already seen, that when Mr. Hooker was in the field of controversy, he was there, not from his own choice or seeking, but in obedience to the summons of duty. And yet, he bore no ill-will to a combatant; he could afterward and always meet him, out of the field of controversy, with all the kindness and courtesy of a christian and a friend. His public dispute with Roger Williams was probably as exciting and difficult as any controversy in which he was at any time engaged. But tradition relates that years afterward when they met, accidentally, Mr. Hooker showed towards his former antagonist, the kindness of friendship, entirely uninfluenced by any thing which had passed between them as controversialists;—and doubtless his feelings were reciprocated by Mr. Williams. Mr. Hooker seems to have been one of those men who had no love for contention; and with whom,—for this reason,—it was very difficult for other men to contend. There is no harder work on earth than to quarrel with a good man who has a good temper. The fighting will have to be all done on one side.

The intercourse of Mr. Hooker with his brethren of the ministry was marked with great cordiality and affection. He loved, as brothers, his fellow-laborers in "the work of Christ." Sometimes he preached his way directly into the hearts of his brethren; and by the freedom and affection of private intercourse, won their affection at others. His first sermon at Delft, in Holland,—whither he had fled from persecution at home,—was on the text, Philippians 1 : 29, "For unto you it is given in the behalf of Christ, not only to believe on him; but also to suffer for his sake;" in which, it would seem that he made his way into the heart of good Mr. Forbes: for "after that sermon, Mr. Forbes manifested a strong desire to enjoy the fellowship of Mr. Hooker in the work of the gospel, which he did about the space of two years; in all which time they lived so like brethren, that an observer might say of them, as was said of Bazil and Nazianzen, 'They were but one soul in two bodies;'

and if they had been any little while asunder, they still met with such friendly and joyful congratulations, as testified a most affectionate satisfaction in each other's company."* So likewise had it been, in his previous residence at Chelmsford, associated with Mr. Mitchell; although there was considerable disparity in the talents of the two men, their labors together were "in a most comfortable amity."†

Such relationships in the work of the ministry, are often attended with considerable delicacy and difficulty. But there are examples such as we have just mentioned, in sufficient number to prove that it is practicable for colleagues in the ministry of one church, to live in entire harmony and affection. Mr. Stone's Letter shows this to be true in his and Mr. Hooker's experience.

Mr. Hooker delighted to bear honorable testimony to the excellence and eminence of his brethren. No feelings of jealous rivalry seemed to make him reserved in speaking of their worth. "*My brother Mather is a mighty man*," said he of Mr. Richard Mather, the ancestor of that family and line of useful men, of the name. Mr. Rogers, of Dedham, England, was, in his

* Magnalia, I. 308. † Ibid, 304.

estimate, and as he expressed himself, "*the prince of all preachers.*" And respecting the intellectual power and productions of his friend, Dr. Ames, he expressed himself in a manner equally full and honorable.

He was worthy of imitation, also, in the kind interest he was accustomed to take in his younger brethren, especially those who were just entering upon the arduous duties of the sacred office. To such he was a wise and affectionate counsellor, as circumstances required. Thomas Shepard gives an illustration of this remark, from his own experience. The question was under consideration, whether Mr. Shepard would do wisely to accept of a Lectureship proposed to him in Cogshall, Essex, England. "Most of the ministers were for it, because it was a great town, and they did not know any place that did desire it but they. Mr. Hooker only did object against my going thither: for being but young and unexperienced, and there being an old but sly and malicious minister in that place, who did seem to give way to it to have it there; he did therefore say it was dangerous for little birds to build under the nests of old ravens and kites."* This advice

* Life of Shepard, p. 114.

kept Mr. Shepard from going to Cogshall, and from difficulty there, doubtless, to which his experience was unequal. He was immediately employed at Tarling, in Essex, under circumstances far more favorable both to his ministerial usefulness and comfort. A letter of Mr. Hooker to Mr. Shepard is preserved in the Library of the Massachusetts Historical Society, in relation to some perplexities in his private affairs, which shows that Mr. Hooker readily and deeply sympathized with a junior brother in his troubles, and offered the best advice in his power.

Mr. Hooker's disinterestedness, already described, gave energy to his generosity and his pious liberality. If the widow needed five pounds, or ten pounds, from his purse, and if he knew of her necessities, she was quite sure to receive it. "His eye affected his heart," and made him ready to do substantial service to the afflicted. Especially if the families of deceased ministers needed his aid, he was ready to impart for their supply. The widow and family of his friend Dr. Ames, who died at Rotterdam, Holland, came to New England to reside. Their house was destroyed by fire; and being reduced to much poverty and affliction, the charitable heart of Mr. Hooker, and others that joined with him, upon advice thereof, comfortably provided for them."* A scarcity of bread-corn was felt at Southampton, (probably on Long Island.) Mr. Hooker united with others in sending to the inhabitants, for their supply, a boat-load of many hundred bushels of corn. He who loved to break to men the "bread of eternal life," was ready also, as occasion required, to dispense that bread which is temporal. He had himself been in a remarkable manner a child of Providence; had been led, protected, "brought forth into a large place," in being brought to such a field of usefulness and of christian privileges as New England. And he held himself ready for all those kind offices to others, which became him, as a child of Providence. It does not appear that he possessed any property, by inheritance from his parents; yet he had a competence, and manifested a liberality equal to that of many who were more wealthy.†

It has already been observed that Mr. Hooker, in his native country, and while in the Church of England, was placed in circumstances which constrained him to give much time and study to the subject of Ecclesiastical Polity; and in this

* Magnalia, I. 309.

† Mr. Hooker's estate was estimated at £1336.15; his Library at £300.

country to employ his pen upon the same subject. Allusion is here again made to this circumstance, preparatory to a few remarks on Mr. Hooker's character as a pastor and administrator of the government of the church.

With all his study of the subject of church government, Mr. Hooker was as far as possible from the love of making laws for Christ's house, for the simple pleasure of administering them, as an exhibition of authority and power. So far as the treatment of offences was concerned, he evidently regarded ecclesiastical law in the light of a system of provisions for exigencies, to which resort might be had, when advice, persuasion, appeals to conscience, in any of the members of the church, had been tried and found insufficient; and relied upon the influence of sound ecclesiastical law, united with kind pastoral influence, as preventive of evil, and anticipating the necessity of disciplinary measures. "He was much troubled at the too frequent censures in some other churches; and he would say, 'Church censures are things wherewith neither we nor our fathers have been acquainted in the practice of them; and therefore the utmost circumspection is needful, that we do not spoil the ordinances of God by our management thereof.'" * A fact will illustrate the importance of his views and his practice, on this subject. During all the years of his pastorship of the Church in Hartford, there occurred *but two cases* in which the steps of discipline for offences against christian law were found necessary.

"He was very careful to have every thing done with christian moderation and unanimity. Wherefore, he would have nothing publicly propounded unto the brethren of the church, but what had been first privately prepared by the elders." † He relied much, and not in vain, upon mutual, clear and good understanding among the members of the church; and promoted this in the friendly interchange of views on points of difficulty, previously, so as to ensure unity of opinion and action when the brethren came together. He never pushed a vote, in the face of agitated and conflicting feelings, but would delay till another meeting; so that opportunity for fraternal consultation and union of minds might prepare the church to act with deliberation and harmony. His own kind and prudent aid to the minds of the brethren of the church, on points which were attended with

* Magnalia, I. 317. † Magnalia, I. 316, 317.

difficulty, and respecting which there was liability to division in sentiment and action, seems to have been instrumental in reconciling differing minds, and relieving perplexities relative to the course of action proper to be pursued when assembled.

The important and responsible work of examining candidates for admission to membership and communion in ordinances, he conducted with great care. He appears to have acted, and taught his church to act, in this important department of duty, upon the principle, that profession of religion, to be safe, must be attested as sincere, by the credible exhibition of the Scripture evidences of a renewed heart, and by a manner of life, holy, in accordance with the precepts of the gospel. He who had seen the deep corruption of the national church of his native land, through the admission of multitudes to membership and ordinances, in disregard of their apparent utter destitution of religion, had thus been most solemnly taught the necessity of watching for the *purity* of the church, by diligently and carefully guarding the *door of admission* into the church.

Of the social character of Mr. Hooker, little is known beyond what appears in such notices as the following: "In conversation he was pleasant and entertaining, but always grave. He was affable, and condescending, and charitable. Yet his appearance and conduct were with such becoming majesty, authority and prudence, that he could do more with a word or a look, than other men would do with a severe discipline." *

This imperfect sketch of Mr. Hooker's character, in some of its principal features, may properly be closed with a reference to the general views of him given by a recent New England historian, who appears to have been a close and accurate student of the characters of American worthies. They indicate the high estimate formed of Mr. Hooker, as prominent among great and good men. After having described Haynes and Cotton, in the grand outlines of their characters, and placing them high among the worthies of their day, this historian proceeds : " and Hooker, of vast endowments, a strong will, and an energetic mind ; ingenuous in his temper, and open in his professions ; trained to benevolence by the discipline of affliction ; versed in tolerance, by his refuge in Holland ; choleric, yet gentle in his affections ; firm in his faith, yet readily yielding to the

* Holmes' Hist. Camb., p. 40.

power of reason; the peer of the reformers, without their harshness; the devoted apostle to the humble and the poor; severe towards the proud; mild in his soothings of a wounded spirit; glowing with the raptures of devotion, and kindling with the messages of redeeming love; his eye, voice, gesture and whole frame animate with the living vigor of heartfelt religion; public spirited and lavishly charitable; and, 'though persecutions and banishments had awaited him, as one wave follows another,' ever serenely blessed with 'a glorious peace of soul;' fixed in his trust in Providence and in his adhesion to that cause of advancing civilization which he cherished always, even while it remained to him a mystery. This was he, whom, for his abilities and services, his cotemporaries placed 'in the first rank' of men; praising him as 'the one rich pearl with which Europe more than repaid America for the treasures from her coast.'" *

* Bancroft's History of the United States, vol. I., pp. 363, 364.

## CHAPTER VII.

Works of Mr. Hooker—reasons for a particular account of them. Titles of his principal works. Surreptitious manner of first publication. Christ his great theme. Theology. Treatment of the experiences of the soul. Instructions to those in an unregenerate state. Instructions to the regenerate ;—on christian duties—christian privileges—christian trials—christian encouragements. Discrimination in characters. Views of the christian ministry.

THE present and a following chapter will be devoted to a particular account of the writings of Mr. Hooker; for the following reasons. They are, in some points, peculiar in their character, as respects many of the subjects of which they treat, and the manner in which those subjects are treated ; and as compared with the writings of his time. They will assist in understanding the true ground of the reputation, which both Puritan and civil history report of his character as a public religious instructor. They are very little known among us, with the exception of one small tractate, none of them having been republished in this country; and of those published in England, none have been printed since 1658, and of course have not been brought into fair contact with the christian mind of New England. With the exception of the single small work to which allusion has been made, Mr. Hooker's works are now very rarely to be found. They are in detached parts, scattered and very carefully shut up, as venerable curiosities, in a very few libraries; to be seen and examined, of course, by those only whose interest in Puritan history and character prompts them to some pains-taking, to find and search into them.

So far as this Series of Lives of the Chief Fathers of New England is designed for the perusal of *ministers*, it is deemed proper to give a particular account of the writings of Mr. Hooker, in this volume; inasmuch as,—with the exception of his work on Church Polity,—his published writings obviously contain the substance of many of his sermons; and as such, they show to the minister of the present time, how a Puritan, of more than two hundred years since, was accustomed to preach. They somewhat help to explain the secret of the wonderful power of his preaching, and that of some of his cotemporaries in New England, respecting which Puritan historians have so unitedly testified.

The rank assigned to Mr. Hooker's writings,

also, by different historians, who have given general statements of their character, is such as to justify particularity in an account of them. As examples of opinions respecting them, President Stiles, in his Literary Diary, remarks, "Mr. Bulkley [supposed to be Peter Bulkley] was a masterly reasoner in theology. I consider him and President Chauncey, Mr. Hooker, Mr. Norton and Mr. Davenport, as the greatest divines among the first ministers of New England; and equal to the first characters in theology in all Christendom and in all ages." * "Mr. Hooker's books," says a cotemporary writer, "are in great request among the faithful people of Christ." † Mr. Hugh Peters, in his "Dying Father's Last Legacy to his Daughter," written in 1660, thus indicates with what order of religious writings he classed those of Mr. Hooker: "Above all things, know that nothing can do you any good without union with Christ the head; which can never be till your understanding be enlightened with the want of Christ and his worth. Read Shepard's Sincere Convert, Daniel Rogers' Practical Catechism, and T. Hooker, to this end, with such other helps as

* Mass. Hist. Col., XX. 260.

† Holmes' Hist. Camb., p. 40.

you may get." Again, "Do but mind in your reading what a sober, plain, unaffected, holy strain is in Dod, Sibbs, Preston, Hooker, Burroughs, &c." And again he speaks of "the love and labors of Mr. Thomas Hooker," by which he had been benefited.*

The author of "Wonder-working Providence of Zion's Saviour, in New England," who has thrown into quaint, but truthful form, his own estimate of the writings of this Father, has these lines, among others, apostrophizing him.†

"Thy golden tongue and pen Christ caused to be
  The blazing of his golden truths profound.
Thou sorry worme, it's Christ wrought this in thee,
  What Christ has wrought must needs be very sound.
Then looke on Hooker's workes, they follow him
  To grave; this worthy resteth there a while;
Die shall he not that hath Christ's warrior been;
  Much less Christ's truth, cleer'd by his people's toile.
Thou angel bright, by Christ for light now made,
  Throughout the world as seasoning salt to be,
Although in dust thy body mouldering fade;
  Thy Head's in heaven, and hath a crown for thee."

A statement of the titles of Mr. Hooker's published writings will prepare the way for the general purpose of the present chapter. As

* Hanb., III. 573.
† Mass. Hist. Col., XIII. 137.

prepared, from the best records to which the writer has found access, they stand as follows:

1. The Soul's Ingrafting into Christ, published in London, 1637.

2. The Soul's Implantation; a Treatise, containing The Broken Heart; The Preparation of the Heart; The Soul's Ingraffing into Christ; Spiritual Love and Joy. Lond. 1637.

3. The Soul's Preparation for Christ. Lond. 1638.

4. The Unbeliever's Preparing for Christ, part I. Lond. 1638.

5. The Unbeliever's Preparing for Christ, part II. Lond. 1638.

6. The Soul's Exaltation; embracing Union with Christ; Benefits of Union with Christ; and Justification. Lond. 1638.

7. Ten Particular Rules, to be practiced every day, by Converted Christians. Lond. 1641.

8. The Soul's Vocation, or Effectual Calling to Christ. Lond. 1638.

9. The Faithful Covenanter; a sermon preached at Dedham, in Essex. Lond. 1644.

10. Survey of the Summe of Church Discipline. Lond. 1648.

11. The Saint's Dignitie and Dutie. Lond. 1651; containing The Gift of Gifts, or why Christ gave himself; The Blessed Inhabitant,

or the Benefit of Christ's being in Believers; Grace Magnified, or the Privileges of those that are under Grace; Wisdom's Attendants, or the Voice of Christ to be obeyed; The Activitie of Faith, or Abraham's Imitators.

12. Culpable Ignorance, or the Danger of Ig norance under Means. Lond. 1651.

13. Wilful Hardness, or the Means of Grace Abused. Lond. 1651.

14. The Application of Redemption, by the Effectual work of the Word and Spirit of Christ, for the bringing home of lost Sinners to God. Lond. 1657.

15. Christ's Prayer for Believers; a Series of Discourses founded on John 17: 20—26. Date supposed, 1657.

16. The Poor Doubting Christian drawn to Christ. Lond. ——. Boston, 1743. Hartford, 1845.

17. Farewell Sermon to his Parish at Chainsford, [Chelmsford,] England.

To this catalogue should be added the titles of a few other books by Mr. Hooker, whose existence is learned only from the advertisements of London booksellers, at dates cotemporaneous with those already mentioned, from 1633 to 1658:—

18. An Exposition of the Lord's Prayer.

19. The Soul's Possession of Christ.

20. The Soul's Justification, Eleven Sermons, on 2 Corinthians 5 : 21.

21. Sermons, on Judges 10 : 23. Psalm 119 : 29. Proverbs 1 : 28, 29. 2 Timothy 3 : 5.

22. The Soul's Humiliation. Luke 15 : 15—18.

23. Farewell to England. Jer. 14 : 9. (This may be the same with No. 17 above.)

The fact appears, incidentally, in some of the prefaces to works of Mr. Hooker, published since his death, that he was averse to authorship; and that it was in part through the urgency of Christian friends he prepared any of his writings for publication. It also happened to Mr. Hooker, as to Mr. Shepard, and perhaps to other Puritan preachers, while in England, that they were followed by note-takers, or stenographers, who wrote down their discourses as preached, and printed them without permission or revision. The motive of such persons, it is most natural to hope, was to do good by the dissemination of the rich instructions with which the discourses abounded, and by which, perhaps, themselves had been edified. And as thus published, even, they might have been useful to the afflicted people of Christ, and to inquirers of that trying period. Their publication, however, in a different way, would have been far preferable; as injustice was sometimes done to Mr. Hooker's views as a preacher, and to his reputation as an author; by inaccuracies in the statement of his sentiments, and in style.

It was some apology for the publication of Mr. Hooker's discourses in this way, that his great aversion to publishing any thing of his own, kept his writings out of the hands of readers, who had not enjoyed the privilege of hearing him in public. The reason of this aversion to authorship does not appear, from any thing he ever said; but is left to be inferred from his obvious indisposition to court notoriety. This is well in itself; but becomes, in effect, a fault, when it interferes with methods of usefulness which are opened by divine providence, and solicited by the spiritual tastes and necessities of Christians. If every good man, with a mind capable of acting on other minds through the press, may yield to his diffidence of authorship, and shut up all the results of his studies and his preaching, in manuscripts as illegible as the few of Mr. Hooker's, which have been preserved; neither the church nor the world are likely to be benefited by his knowledge and attainments, after he is gone to his grave.

Mr. Hooker's preparation of any thing of his own for the press, therefore, seems to have been done under the pressure of two things. First, he was liable to all the mortifications and misapprehensions attendant on surreptitious publication by others, and he knew not whom. Second, his friends importuned him, with an urgency which he could not very well withstand. To these two causes, and to the fact that a considerable number of his sermons were copied by Mr. Higginson, (Mather says about 200,) after his death, and sent to England for publication, it is owing, that even so many of his works have appeared as are now in existence.

The work entitled, "The Application of Redemption," is one which Mr. Hooker prepared for the press with his own hand; and in point of finish is far in advance of several others of his works. The "Epistle to the Reader" having the signatures of Thomas Goodwin and Philip Nye, two eminent men of the time, in the Puritan ranks, contains the following passages:—"And whereas there have been published, long since, many parts and pieces of this author upon this argument, sermon-wise preached by him here in England, (which in the preaching of them did enlighten all those parts,) yet having been taken by an unskilful hand, which upon his recess into those remote parts of the world, was bold, without his privity or consent, to print and publish them, (one of the greatest injuries which can be done to any man,) it came to pass that his genuine meaning, and this in points of so high a nature, and in some things differing from the common opinion, was diverted in those printed sermons from the fair and cleer draught of his own notions and intentions; because so utterly deformed and misrepresented in multitudes of passages; and in the rest but imperfectly and crudely set forth.

"Here, in these treatises thou hast his heart from his own hand; his own thoughts drawn by his own pencil. *This is all truly and purely his own, not as preached only, but as written by himself,* in order to the press; which may be a great satisfaction to all that honored and loved him, (as who that was good, and knew him, did not?) especially those that received benefit by those other imperfect editions. And we cannot but look at it as a blessed Providence of God, that the publishing of the same by others, (in that manner that hath been mentioned,) should have provoked him, and that by the excitation of the church, (whereof he was the pastor in *New England,*) to go over again the same materials in the course of his ministry amongst them; in order to the perfecting of it by his own hand for publick light; thereby to vindicate both himself and it from that wrong which otherwise had remained forever irrecompensible. And hereby it came to pass, (that so far as he hath proceeded,) this subject come to have a *third concoction* in the heart and head of him that was one of the most experienced Christians and of acutest abilities that have been living in our age. He *preached* more briefly of this subject, *first*, while he was Fellow and Catechist in Emmanuel College, in Cambridge. The notes of which, were then so much esteemed, that many copies thereof were by many that heard not the sermons, written out, and are yet extant by them. And then again, a second time, many yeers after, more largely, at Great Chelmsford in Essex; the product of which, was those books of sermons that have gone under his name. And last of all; *now* in *New England*, and that in and to a *settled church* of saints, to which the promise is made of being '*The Seat and Pillar of Truth;*' and in which all ordinances set as the load-stone in the steel, have the greater power and energie; in which the presence of Christ breaks forth, and all his springs are found therein."

In the same volume with the foregoing, and with a prefatory epistle to the reader, having the same signatures, is published Mr. Hooker's series of discourses upon the latter portion of our Saviour's Intercessory Prayer, John 17 : 20—26. These were preached, as appears from the preface, towards the close of his life, on occasions of the administration of the Lord's Supper. The principal object of these discourses was, to present that great and interesting subject, the spiritual union of believers with Christ. It is remarked, in the prefatory epistle, "And indeed he that is spiritual, and reads these explanations, will readily find, and must acknowledge, that he was proportionably raised and assisted by a Gospel Spirit, as the dignity of the matter and the solemnity of the occasion, meeting in such conjunction, did require; it being found in experience, that according to the elevation of the occasion, and sublimity of the matter discoursed of, the Holy Ghost raiseth and enlargeth the spirits of an holy man of God, that is experienced in what he speaks."

From the above statement, and an attentive examination of the discourses to which it refers, it is to be inferred that Mr. Hooker was accustomed to make that "*high day,*" *the sacramental Sabbath*, a season of profit to the people of

Christ, by rich instructions relating to Him; and eminently adapted to make the Lord's Supper a season of spiritual refreshment and delight. Amidst the sweet solemnities of that scene, where "*the love of Christ*" is celebrated; if his administration of the ordinance was in keeping with the preaching which preceded it, preparation of the hearts of Christians around him must have been made, for each to retire, at the conclusion, saying, with tenderness and emphasis, of Him whose love prepared the feast, "I sat down under his shadow with great delight, and his fruit was sweet to my taste."

These discourses also are commended to the reader by the writers of the prefatory epistle, assuring him, "*that they are all as they were penned under his own hand;* praying with all earnestness, that the Holy Spirit of Christ, who dwelt in the author so richly, and blessed his preaching of them with so much life and power; yea, that filled our Saviour Christ's heart first in his praying and uttering these words; and then his beloved disciples so may years after in the penning of them; would graciously accompany this quickening and heavenly exposition of them, to the hearts of all spiritual souls who read this."*

* Preface to the work.

Two other collections of Mr. Hooker's discourses were prepared from his manuscripts, as they were left in his own hand-writing, and certified to be genuine in the prefatory epistles; one of them by Thomas Goodwin and Philip Nye, dated June 26, 1656, and the other still earlier, in 1651, having a preface signed with the initials " *T. S.*," probably Thomas Shepard, his son-in-law, and his successor at Newtown.

The rest of Mr. Hooker's published writings appeared without any intimations, by preface or otherwise, of the editorship under which they were brought forward; with the exception of his "Poor Doubting Christian drawn to Christ." The American edition of this book, published more than a hundred years since, (1743,) in Boston, appeared with a brief sketch of his life, by Rev. Thomas Prince; and from this was printed the Hartford edition of 1845.

In proceeding to consider the characteristics of Mr. Hooker's writings, we first notice the fact, which is discoverable by a glance at the catalogue of them, already given, that *Christ Jesus was his grand theme.* He contemplates the soul in various relations to Christ; its "Preparation for Christ;" "Vocation or Effectual Calling to Christ;" "Union with Christ;" "Ingrafting into Christ;" "Drawn to Christ." The spirit which led him thus to keep the Great Redeemer before the eyes of his hearers and the readers of these works, also pervades his writings upon other subjects, the *titles* of which do not contain the name of Christ. The Saviour of lost men was "all and in all," with him. It was remarked of him, by an early historian of New England,—"Although he had a notable hand at the discussing and adjusting of controversial points, yet he would hardly ever handle any polemical divinity in the pulpit. But the very spirit of his ministry lay in the points of the most practical religion in the grand concerns of a sinner's preparation for, implantation in, and salvation by the glorious Lord Jesus Christ."*

Nor does it appear, in the examination of his published writings, that Mr. Hooker was often accustomed to bring forward and discuss theological positions as such, and in the way of system. Perhaps this was a defect; but if so, there was ample atonement made for it, in the other excellencies of his preaching. His subjects appear to have been chosen with reference to meeting the peculiar wants of his christian hearers and others, arising out of the exigencies

* Magnalia, I, 314.

of the times, and the trials, inward and outward, which were experienced by the people of God with whom he became acquainted.

And yet Mr. Hooker's theology was sound in every point; and his positions wherever given, of a doctrinal character, were set in unquestionable clearness. There is not a sentence in all his writings, which he prepared for the press himself, nor in those published by others, interpreted by the general scope of his works, which contains the slightest savor of Arminianism, Pelagianism, Antinomianism, or any other like errors. It is impossible for the attentive and discriminating reader to fail of discerning, that on all the great and fundamental doctrines of the Scriptures, as understood, believed and taught by the strong men among the Puritan divines, and by the soundest theologians of the present age, he was firmly established. No man, indeed, can treat such deep subjects of christian experience as he discussed, and do it with such skill, thoroughness and adaptation to the varied vicissitudes of the christian life, as appear upon his pages, without being a firm believer in the entire depravity of man by nature; his helpless dependence upon "the power of the Spirit of God," and the necessity of his regeneration by the Holy Spirit; the sovereignty of

God in the dispensation of grace to guilty men; the deity of Christ, and of the Holy Spirit; and all the truths which concern man's deliverance from sin and woe growing out of these; the atonement of Christ, as the only satisfaction to divine justice on man's behalf; justification by faith alone, and the imputation of the righteousness of Christ; the justice of God in his final and eternal retributions upon sinners who reject the salvation offered in Christ Jesus; and the unspeakable grace of God, in the bestowment of eternal life upon the heirs of salvation. These and all the other great truths, which in more recent times have been denominated by the various terms, "Orthodox," "Calvinistic," "the doctrines of the Reformation," "Old Divinity," constitute the basis of Mr. Hooker's writings; and impart to them a richness, seriousness and most searching power upon the conscience and the heart. His writings are a mass of enigmas, if he did not fully believe these great first truths of the christian system. And his habit of studying the condition and necessities of men as sinners, and of those who had entered upon the christian life, was obviously in connection with these high and holy truths; and with reference to their efficient instrumentality, through the power of the divine Spirit, in man's salvation from sin and death.

Mr. Hooker was accustomed to treat much of the experiences of the soul, both as they appeared before and after regeneration, and in the progress of christian sanctification. He studied the unregenerate heart, as well as the heart of the new man in Christ Jesus. As an example of the former, take the treatise with the impressive title, "A Treatise upon Contrition; wherein is discovered how God breaks the heart and wounds the soul in the conversion of a sinner to himself.* His pages abound with passages which are strikingly descriptive of the endlessly diversified exercises of an unregenerate mind; from those of a state of insensibility to eternal things, through all the workings of thought and feeling under awakening, fear, conviction of sin, and conflict with the truths and claims of God, and with the conditions of the salvation of the gospel. He shows himself familiar with the innumerable cavils and subterfuges of an unregenerate heart; with every objection, and every form of self-delusion and hypocrisy which the sinner practices upon himself and his fellow

* The same noticed in the list of his works, called "The Soul's Preparation for Christ."

men, and with which he seeks to elude the claims of a righteous God. And he even contemplates and by Scripture light analyzes the experiences of the lost and the despairing in the world of woe ; and shows not only what are the present elements of the sinner's unhappiness, on this side of the grave, but what will be the fearful elements of that wretchedness which will overwhelm the ungodly in eternity.

And then, when he treats of the regenerate soul, he appears to have read the history of the experiences of all the saints who have ever reached heaven ; and to have studied them, from the first emotions of christian hope, up to the highest raptures of the dying hour of the believer in Jesus ; and then to have followed on, by Scripture light, into the scenes of heavenly bliss ; and to have contemplated their bliss as consisting in being where Christ is, and beholding the glory of God in heaven.

At every step in his discussions of christian duty and experience, he appears acquainted with the ever varying circumstances of the christian life, and like Bunyan's "Mr. Greatheart," to know how to counsel pilgrims of all varieties of christian temperament, on the way to "the Celestial City." Not many writers on christian experience equal him, in treating this class of subjects; and none surpass him, in the richness of scriptural instruction, in which he spreads them out before the minds of his readers, and awakens the deep feelings of their hearts, incites them to seek the communications of the Spirit for their advancement in holiness.

But it will be important to the object of the present volume, to show more particularly the manner in which Mr. Hooker was accustomed to instruct the two great classes of men; those in an unregenerate state, and those in a state of grace and of progressive sanctification.

In the instructions which he gives to those who are yet in a state of unregeneracy, it is evidently his great object to bring God and the sinner together,—or, more properly, to bring the sinner to be "reconciled to God," and to enter upon the way of eternal life. In doing this, however, he takes high ground, in behalf of God, as holy, just, merciful, sovereign. With the utmost fidelity of an "ambassador for Christ," he advocates every claim of the divine holiness upon the sinner; lays upon his conscience and his heart the tremendous weight of the divine law, and the dread responsibility of all his transgressions, and of his final destruction, if he perishes. He leaves nothing untried in the way of argument on the side of God, which love to the divine character and jealousy for the divine honor could prompt him to plead with the sinner's conscience. He applies himself, with directness and pungency unsparing, to the unregenerate man, respecting the manifestations of his impenitence, in whatever form they appear. Having studied the soul in its unregeneracy, by light shining from the glory of the divine character, he gives the results of his studies, in faithful endeavors to help the man to see himself by the same light. In relation to conviction of sin by the divine law, his views were of the same character with those which have been entertained and acted upon by New England ministers, in the revivals which President Edwards describes, and in those which occurred during the first quarter of the present century.

The foregoing remarks will be best understood, with the aid of a few illustrative extracts, upon topics which can be named.

"*What the true sight of sin is.* It is not every sight of sin will serve the turn, nor every apprehension of a man's vileness; but it must have these two properties. First, he must see sin clearly: Secondly, convictingly. He that will see sin clearly, must see it truly and fully, and be able to fathom the depth of his corruptions, and to dive into the depths of the wretchedness of his vile heart. Otherwise it will befall a man's sin as it doth the wound of a man's body: when a man looks into the wound overly,* and doth not search it to the bottom, it begins to fester and wranckle; and so, in the end he is slain by it. So it is with most sinners. We carry all away with this, 'We are sinners,' and such ordinary confessions; but we never see the depth of the wound of sin, and so are slain by our sins. It is not enough to say, 'It is my infirmity, and I cannot mend it;' and 'We are all sinners.' A man must prove his ways as a goldsmith doth his gold, in the fire; must search narrowly, and must have light to see what the vileness of his own heart is, and what his sins are that do procure the wrath of God against him. As David saith, 'I thought on my ways and turned my feet unto thy testimonies;' the phrase in the original is, 'I turned my sins upside down. He looked over all his ways. And Zechariah saith, 'They shall look on me whom they have pierced and shall mourn for him as one mourneth for an only son, and shall be in bitterness for him as one that is in bitterness for his first born.'

"We must look upon the nature of sin, in the

* Superficially, slightly.

venom of it; the deadly hurtful nature that it hath, for plagues and miseries it doth procure to our souls. Compare sin with those things that are most fearful and horrible. As, suppose any soul here present were to behold the damned in hell, and if the Lord should give thee a little peep-hole into hell, that thou didst see the horror of those damned souls, and thy heart begins to shake in the consideration thereof, then propound this to thine own heart, 'what pains the damned in hell do endure for sin!' and thine heart shall shake and quake at it. The least sin that ever thou didst commit, though thou makest a light matter of it, is a greater evil than the pains of the damned in hell, setting aside their sin. All the torments in hell are not so great an evil as the least sin is. Men begin to shrink at this, and loathe to go down to hell and to be in endless torments."

"*What a horrible thing sin is.* That which deprives a man of the greatest good, must needs be the greatest evil. The good of the soul is, to have a heart united unto God, and to have fellowship with him, and salvation through him: to be one with God is the chiefest good of the soul. It is sin that breaks the union between God and us,—'Your sins have separated between you and your God.' It is not punishment that takes away the mercy of God from us; but a proud rebellious heart, and the contempt of God's ordinances. There is nothing so contrary and opposite against the Lord, as sin and corruption; and this is the reason why God is the inflicter of all the punishments of the damned in hell. Sin doth procure all plagues and punishments to the damned; and therefore being the cause why they suffer, it must needs be greater than all punishments. For all punishments are made miserable by sin, therefore sin is a greater evil than all the miseries of the damned. Let us look upon sin through these things; and when our corrupt heart provokes us, and the world allures us, and the devil tempts us to take any contentment in a sinful way; suppose we saw hell fire burning before us, and the pit of hell gaping to swallow us; and sin enticing us. And let us say thus to our souls, 'it is better for a man to be cast into the torments of hell among the damned, than to be overcome with any sin, and so to rebel against the Lord. Were a man in hell and wanted * his sins, the Lord would love him in hell, and deliver him from all those plagues. But if any man were free from all punishments, and in honour and wealth; if he

* Was without.—Ed.

were a sinful and wretched creature, the Lord would hate him in the height of all his prosperity, and throw him down to hell forever."

"*How to see our sins convictingly.* This is the cursed distemper of our hearts, howsoever we hold it to be truth in general, yet when we come to our own sins the case is altered, and we never come to the right seeing of them, as they concern our own particular. Arrest thy soul in a special manner of those sins whereof thou standest guilty. That phrase in Job is to good purpose ; 'Thou lookest narrowly to my paths, thou settest a print upon the heels of my feet.' As God followed Job to the hard heels, and did so narrowly observe his ways, so deal thou with thine own soul ; and set a print upon the heel of thine heart. Arrest thy heart in particular for thy sins. Follow them to your hearts, and make a hue and cry after your sins, and drag your hearts before the Lord, and say, 'Is murder, pride, drunkenness and uncleanness such horrible sin, and doth God thus fearfully plague them ? Lord, it was mine heart that was proud and vain: it was my tongue that did speak filthily and blasphemously. My hand hath wrought wickedness : my eye was wanton and my heart was unclean and filthy. Lord here they are. It is my affections that are disorderly, and it is I that do delight too much in the world.' Thus bring thou thy heart before the Lord. Play thou the part of Nathan, and say, 'I am the man.' The soul must be set down with the audience of the truth, and the conscience of a sinner should be so convicted as to yield and give way to that which is known; as not seeking any shift or way to oppose that truth which is revealed. This particular apprehension of sin is like the indictment of the sinner before God; and his conviction is that which brings the soul to such a pass that the heart will not,—nay, it does not,—nay, which is more,—it cannot escape from the truth revealed.

"We must go to God for knowledge. The Lord knows our hearts; therefore we must go to him, that he will make us able to know them too.

"If any stubborn heart shall say, 'God is merciful, and therefore we may live as we list,' take heed; that just law that hath been contemned, and those righteous statutes that have been broken, and God that hath been provoked by you, will be revenged of you. Did ever any provoke the Lord and prosper, and shall you begin? Where is Nimrod, and Nebuchadnezzar and Pharaoh and Herod, and those proud persons that set their mouths against God and their hearts against heaven ; what is now become of them? They are now in the lowermost pit of hell. God sent Pharaoh into the Red Sea ; and for aught we know his soul may now be roaring in hell. This is certain that whosoever resisteth God, shall find him a swift Judge to condemn him.

" You know not your sins ; therefore get you home to the law, and look into the glass thereof, and then bundle up all your sins thus ; 'So many sins against God himself in the first commandment ; against his worship in the second ; against his name in the third ; against his Sabbath in the fourth commandment. Nay, all our thoughts, words and actions, all have been sins, able to sink our souls to the bottom of hell. Those sins of thine were the witnesses against our Saviour : they were the soldiers that took him, the thorns that pierced him, the spear that gored him, the cross that took away his life. The soldiers and Pilate and the Scribes and Pharisees could have done nothing to our Saviour but for thy sins. Thy sins caused all this ; thy wicked thoughts and wicked actions caused our Saviour to cry out, 'My God, my God, why hast thou forsaken me!' "

" *Sins of the thoughts and imagination.* Look at thoughts in regard to the other evils of our lives, which are acted and appear in our daily course. We may thus come to take a guess at the greatness of the evil of our thoughts. For it will appear they are the causes of all other evils. And therefore it cannot be doubted there is more and worse evil in them than in all the rest. A man's imaginations are the forge of villany, where it is all framed ; the ware-house of wickedness, the magazine of all mischief and iniquity, where the sinner is furnished to the commission of all evil in all his ordinary course; the sea of abominations, which overflows into all the senses; and they are polluted in all the parts of the body ; and they are defiled and carried aside with many noisome corruptions. 'Out of the heart proceed evil thoughts, murders, adulteries, fornications, thefts, false-witness, blasphemies; these are the things that defile a man.' There is the nest where all these noisome vermin are bred.—The imagination of our mind is the great wheel, that carries all with it; that loathsome and execrable wickedness, worse than which the sun never saw, the earth never bore, (the unpardonable sin excepted). The killing of the Lord Jesus, the Lord of life, the seed of it was a thought cast into the heart of Judas by Satan, (John 13 : 3.) It was warmed by a covetous disposition, and so brought forth that hideous treachery, the betraying of the Lord Jesus.

"Look at the large extent of this spiritual wickedness of the mind, which cannot be bounded; the unavoidableness, it cannot be prevented; and in both we shall see and be forced to confess the aggravations of this evil. There is a compass wherein a man's *words* and *actions* may be confined; he cannot vent the venom of his words, or express his poisonous practices among all men; not among many, many times; but there are no limits nor bounds to be set to the *thoughts of a man's mind*, or the *lusts and desires of the heart*. As the evils of our whole course have their rise and cause from our thoughts, so they are nourished also hereby. Our imaginations are the womb where wickedness is conceived. So are they also the breasts and dugs where they are maintained and nursed up. The sinews of the strength of our distempers lie in the lustings of our mind and heart. When the soul sucks the sweet of a distemper by daily meditation, lies at the dug as it were, and draws out the spirits and quintessence of any noisome lusts and temptations, by daily attendance bestowing his mind and thoughts thereupon, whence the soul comes to be incorporated into a lust and wholly under the power of it. So that the evils be not outward and scandalous; yet it becomes more heinous in the sight of God." "The prophets advice to Jerusalem when he would have her cleansed and saved, directs her to dislodge her vain thoughts; 'O Jerusalem, wash thine heart from wickedness, that thou mayest be saved. How long shall thy vain thoughts lodge within thee?' These vain thoughts are those carnal reasonings, whereby the sinner would put by the authority of the truth, that so the sinner might neither see the loathsomeness of his sin, nor the danger of his estate, or the necessity to recover himself out of it. And if these thoughts lodge within him, there will be no entertainment for the power of any ordinance or counsel that will take place with him, nor reproof awe, nor exhortation persuade. He casts out and keeps off any necessity to be washed and so to be saved. If then, by those vain thoughts thy heart is estranged from God, and carried in opposition against him; if they be the cause of all sins committed and continued in; if the hindrance of all means that might procure our good; then is their evil exceeding henious, and therefore we shonld so judge it, and so be effected with it."

" *How the soul labours to beat back the pow-*

*er of the word.* The soul hath a slight apprehension of sin, and thinketh that it is not so heinous and so dangerous as these hot-spirited ministers bear men in hand. This is usually the common conceit of all men, naturally, and even of us all, more or less to make a slight account of sin,—'What,' saith one, 'are not all sinners as well as we? Though we have many failings, yet we have many fellows.' 'O, all the world lies in sin, and we do no more than the world doth.' 'Are not all sinful by nature, and are not some saved? And why not I as well as others?' 'What, would you have us saints on earth?' Thou sayest true, indeed, thou hast many fellows in thy sins; and thou shalt have share with many fellows in the punishment of thy sins. There is room enough in hell, for thee and all thy fellows. Hell hath opened her mouth wide. Nay, the more companions thou hast had in thy sins, the more shall be thy plagues. What a senseless thing to be such an one as God hates. Is this all thy pleasure, that thou art a hater of God?" "Christ never prayed for the world, and he will never save the world,"—"No man is saved by nature, but if any be saved, the Lord opens his eyes and breaks his heart; and so it must be with thee too, if ever thou thinkest to receive any mercy from God. Dost thou say it is thy nature to sin? then I say, the greater is thy wickedness. Therefore, rather mourn the more for thy sins, because it is thy cursed nature so to do. And say, 'Lord, did only temptations, or the world allure me to this, there were some hope that thou wouldest have mercy upon me; but, O Lord, I have a cursed nature. And though there were no Devils, no world, no temptations outwardly; yet, this cursed nature of mine would sin against thee.'"

*How to meet the pride of human ability.* "If God be so mighty, (say they,) that he knows all, and will call us to account for all; then it is but sorrowing so much the more; and that we will do afterwards; and this will make all well enough, it is but repenting." Be not deceived, God is not, nay, cannot be, mocked, and therefore delude not your own souls. Every repentance will not serve the turn. Thou mayest have remorse of heart and repent and cry to God for thy sins. And this tormenting of thy heart will be but a forerunner of thy everlasting damnation hereafter. The Lord may deal with thee, as Moses said of the people of Israel, "ye returned and wept before the Lord, but he would not hear your voice." So the time may come that all weeping and wailing will not serve the turn. Judas had marvellous horrors of conscience; he took shame to himself and made restitution; and yet a damned creature for ever. Dost thou think thou hast repentance at command? This is that which cuts the throat of men's souls, and deprives them of all the benefit of means of grace. If thou didst consider thy own weakness, then thou wouldst not say that repentance is in thine own power. Remember what the apostle saith, 'If God, peradventure will give them repentance, to the acknowledging of the truth, and that they may recover themselves out of the snare of the devil who are taken captive by him at his will.' It is only *peradventure.* It is a rare work, and few have it."

The secret of the solemnity, pungency, and earnestness with which Mr. Hooker was accustomed thus to apply himself to men, whom he would disturb in their sins, and bring to a just acquaintance with their own characters, is accounted for, when we find him,—with his eye upon Scriptures which teach the aggravated guilt of men's unbelief,—saying, "I must confess, that the consideration of these passages sometimes makes the soul of a poor minister to shake within him." Truly, he was one who sympathized with that prophet who said, "But his word was in my heart as a burning fire shut up in my bones, and I was weary with forbearing and I could not stay." With such conceptions as his, of the deep guilt of sin in man, and of holiness and justice in God against whom it is committed, and of his fearful majesty and might in punishing it; his preaching might well be arousing, humbling and overpowering to the sinner in his impenitence.

Here should be noticed Mr. Hooker's explanation of his reasons for thus solemnly and urgently dealing with unregenerate men. Noticing the objection, "Some will say, if I do thus deal plainly with them, I shall discourage them altogether;" he says, "Nay, but it will make them sound christians. See what the Lord saith; 'Plead with your mother;' the word in the original is, 'call her into court and call her by her name.' And the Lord saith by Ezekiel, 'Cause Jerusalem to know her abominations.' The reasons for acting on such examples and instructions as these, he gives; 'because the word thus applied hits sooner than otherwise it would. Overly discourses, that men are great sinners, and the like, are like the confused noise that was in the ship when Jonah was asleep in it; which never troubled him till at last the master came and said, 'Awake, O sleeper, and call upon thy God;' and, as a Father observes, 'they came about him, and every man had a blow at him, and then did he awake.' The word of God particularly applied sinks deepest. 'The words of the wise are as goads and as nails fastened by the masters of assemblies.'"

Here we see a reason why plain teaching finds so much opposition. "That which works and troubles most, that they most distaste; that which gives the least quiet to them, to that they give the least respect and liking. Some men love vain and windy discourses, to please sinful humors and corrupt hearts; rather than some bitter and particular reproofs which will make them sound in the faith. Ahab will nourish four hundred false prophets at his table, and make choice provision for them, that they may feed his humor, and speak good things to him; when he is not able to abide the sight, scarce to hear the name, of Micaiah the prophet of the Lord, who would speak the counsel of the Lord without fear and partiality, 1 Kings, 22. So they in Isaiah 30: 10. 'Which say to the seers, see not, and to the prophets, prophesy not unto us right things, speak unto us smooth things, prophesy deceits;' so as might suit their several appetites and would go down without chewing. And it is strange to see, when such men have told a grave tale, and vented a heartless, toothless discourse, neither pith nor power in it; I say it is strange to see what admiration and esteem such carnal hearts will set upon such persons and expressions; 'great their parts, prudence and discretion;' 'Oh how sweet and seasonable their discourse;' how glad to hear, and how unweariable to attend such. And all the while they may sit and sleep in their sinful condition, and neither have their consciences awakened, nor their corruption discovered. This is the disease of which Paul complains, as incident to the last age of the world; and therefore adviseth his scholar, Timothy, 'Be instant in season, out of season, reprove, rebuke, exhort, with all long suffering and doctrine; for the time will come when they will not endure sound doctrine; but after their own lusts shall they heap up to themselves teachers, having itching ears;' itching ears that must be scratched, not boxed."

Mr. Hooker, in his conceptions and descriptions of the scenes of the judgment and of eternity, as they are to be presented to the mind of the sinner, is unsurpassed, in solemnity, by any preacher of his day. Leading the sinner forward to the great and final day of judgment, he points him to the fearful array of the divine attributes against him. "Methinks I see the Lord of heaven and earth, and the attributes of God appearing before him. The mercy of God, the goodness of God, the wisdom of God, the power of God, the patience and long suffering of God; and they come all to a sinner, or wicked hypocrite, or a carnal professor, and say,— 'Bounty hath kept you; patience hath borne with you; long-suffering hath endured you; mercy hath relieved you; the goodness of God hath been great unto you.' All these comfortable attributes will say,—'Farewell damned soul; you must go hence to hell, to have fellowship with damned ghosts.' Mercy shall never be enlarged towards you any more. You will never have patience any more to bear with you; never goodness more to screen you; never power more to strengthen you. Nay, you that have heretofore withdrawn yourselves from God's wisdom and gospel; you shall never have wisdom more to guide you; never gospel more to comfort you; never mercy more to cheer you. You shall then go into endless and ceaseless torments. There you shall never be refreshed, never eased, never comforted. And then you shall remember your sins; 'my covetousness and pride was the cause of this; I may thank my sins for this!'"

With like solemnity he gives to the sinner most vivid and awful descriptions of the agonies which await him hereafter. Noticing that plea of unbelieving men, respecting future misery,— "If we cannot avoid it, then we are resolved to bear it as we may;" he proceeds to reply,— "Judge the torments of hell by some little beginning of it, and the dregs of God's vengeance by some little sips of it; and judge how unable thou art to bear the whole, by thy inability to bear a little of it in this life, in the terror of conscience. As the wise man saith, 'a wounded spirit who can bear?' When God lays the flushes of hell fire upon thy soul, thou canst not endure it. Whatsoever a *man* can inflict upon a poor wretch may be borne. But when the *Almighty* comes in battle array against a poor soul, how can he undergo it? Witness the saints that have felt it; as also witness the wicked themselves that have had beginnings of hell in their consciences. When the Lord hath let in a little horror of heart into the soul of a poor sinful creature, how he is transported with an insupportable burden. When it is day, he wisheth it were night, and when it is night, he wisheth it were day. All the friends in the world cannot comfort him. Nay, many have sought to hang themselves; to do any thing rather than to suffer a little vengeance of the Almighty. And one man is roaring and yelling as if he were in hell already, and admits of no comfort. If the drops be so heavy, what will the whole sea of God's vengeance be? If he cannot bear the one, how can he bear the other?"

"*The reason why a sinner never comes out of hell.* A poor creature bearing God's anger, he hath not only God's anger seizing upon him, but also it overwhelms him, because he is not able to bear it. The plague prevails against him. Not only the wrath of God lies upon a sinner in hell, but it crusheth him there, that he can never go from it. And this, divines call the absolute damnation; such a damnation as overturns a sinner in hell, and crusheth him there forevermore. The reason why a sinner never comes out of hell is this: because his sufferings are not infinitely satisfiable here, according as his sins have been infinite to provoke God. For as Adam's sin was infinite and provoking, because it was against the Godhead, so the sufferings must be infinite. Now the sufferings of Christ were of infinite value; but Adam's sufferings were not of an infinite nature. Christ bore the wrath of God, and wrestled with it, and overcame it, and came out from under the heavy displeasure of God, and why? Because his sufferings were able to satisfy an infinite God, who was thus infinitely wronged by the sin of man. Therefore the sufferings must be of an infinite satisfying nature, as you shall conceive thus: a finite sin of Adam, committed against God, was infinitely provoking; but the sufferings of Christ were infinitely satisfying; and so answerable in proportion to what divine justice required. This is the meaning of that place in Acts 2 : 24. 'Whom God hath raised up, having loosed the pains of death, because it was not possible that he should be holden of it;' and of that,—1 Cor. 15 : 54,—'death is swallowed up in victory.' Christ endures wrath and overcomes it. Why did he 'go unto the Father?' Because he has paid the debt to the uttermost. He did satisfy justice to the full; for had he not satisfied justice he had been kept in the grave till this day, and we had been condemned. But now he hath borne and satisfied all; therefore he must come forth to immortality and glory. Remember these conclusions; and think, thus, 'hath my Saviour done all this for me? well I will think upon it and lay it by me forever.'"

Mr. Hooker's writings abound in passages such as have been thus far quoted; indicating that he spared no endeavors to help unrenewed men to conceive of their fearful state of danger on this side of the grave; and of their unutterable woes hereafter, if they pass the gates of death without grace and hope. He studied "the faithful word," as giving faithful warnings to the rejecter of the grace which is in Christ Jesus; and evidently regarded it as an indispensable part of a minister's work, that he should make known "the terrors of the Lord."

And yet, this was only the beginning of what Mr. Hooker aimed and endeavored to do, that he might "persuade men," and win sinners to repentance and to Christ. As an example, he takes for a text, Acts 2 : 37, "Now when they heard this, they were pricked in their heart, and said unto Peter and the rest of the apostles, Men and brethren, what shall we do?" He raises from it this doctrine:—"It is possible for the most stubborn sinner on earth to get a broken heart." And while he most solemnly shows that the condition of every sinner is little short of utter desperation; yet, he addresses himself to the "pricked in heart," great though his guilt be; teaches him, most tenderly and delightfully, "Christ is all-sufficient in power to procure mercy for all thy sins; and the Spirit is all-sufficiently able to apply the satisfaction of Christ to thy soul. And, therefore, be thy condition never so fearful, (the sin against the Holy Ghost only, excepted,) there is power and mercy to pardon thee, and it is possible for thee to find mercy." Earnestly, solemnly, yea terribly, as he sounds in the ears of the sinner the alarms of the law, and aims to help, most efficiently, his conceptions, to the utmost liveliness and terribleness, of the danger and misery of his present condition, and of what will be his future woes; so earnestly, also, and affectionately, does he reason with him on his duties; the divine provision for his help, and of his opportunities of probation; and meets and answers all his objections, whether originating in skepticism, or in discouragement, or in despair at the sight of his amazing guilt. There are no difficulties, in the way of the sinner's persuasion to come to Christ, which he does not endeavor thoroughly to obviate; so that he shall see himself without excuse, if he fail of finding his way to God through Christ Jesus. These general remarks will be illustrated by a few examples.

"We may here take notice of the marvellous tenderness and the loving nature of God, in dealing with poor sinners, [yet in probation,] that in all his courses of justice he remembers some mercy; and in all the potions of his wrath, still he drops in some cordials of comfort. He deals not with us as he might, but so as might be most comfortable every way, and useful to work upon our hearts, and to draw our souls home unto himself. Should the Lord come out against a sinner, and his wrath let fly against him, his soul would sink down under him. But blessed be God that he doth not deal with our hearts as we deserve. If he were as rigorous against us as we have been rebellious against him, we should sink in sorrow and fall into despair, never to be recovered any more."

In dealing with the unregenerate man, he remembers that one of the devices of the devil, when the sinner is shown his exceeding wickedness, is, to tempt him to despair of the divine mercy. "These two be the special extremes, that the devil seeks to drive a man into. If a man presume of his own sufficiency and thinks he is well enough, he will not go to Christ, because he thinks he stands in no need of him. And if he despair of forgiveness by Christ, he will not go to Christ. The soul despairs out of stoutness of heart, because it hath not sufficiency in itself, it will not look out for help and comfort from another. Presumption saith, 'I have sufficiency in myself, and need not go to Christ;' and despair saith, 'I have no sufficiency, and, therefore, will not go to Christ.' Here is the property of despair, to cast away all hope, when a man hath no hope that God will help him. Now all the while the soul looks for sufficiency in Christ, there is hope, for though our sins be never so heinous, that is nothing; all the question is, whether we can hope in Christ. For if all the sins that ever were, are, or shall be committed, ran into one man, as all rivers run into one sea; Christ could as easily pardon his sins, as ever he pardoned the sins of any saints in heaven. A despairing heart is a proud and stubborn heart; because he cannot have what he would of his own, therefore he will not go to another to receive it, and so sinks down in his sins. Therefore, let this be the period and stint of meditation; when the soul so far seeth sin and the punishment deserved by it, that the heart is resolved that none but Christ can take away these sins and the punishments due to them, and is resolved to seek to Christ and to be beholden to him for all; when it is thus with you, then away to the Lord Jesus Christ, and let this meditation of a man's corruptions be as a bridge to carry him to Christ, so that he may have salvation which is promised through him, and shall be bestowed upon all broken-hearted sinners. And mark what I say: that soul that will not seek out to Christ, and will not be beholden to Christ for what he needs; that soul wants brokenness of heart."

"Take heed of that fearful and inconceivable sin of despair. Despair we must in ourselves, and that is good; but this despair we now speak of is marvellous heinous in the eyes of God, and marvellous hurtful to thy own soul. Therefore take heed of it forever, I say,—this sin of despair. Cast away all carnal confidence thou must do, and yet thou must hope; 'Let Israel hope in the Lord, for with the Lord there is mercy, and with him is plenteous redemption.' O, the Lord taketh this very ill at our hands. Thou goest down to the deep dungeon of thy corruption; and there thou sayest, 'These sins can never be pardoned; I am still proud and more stubborn; this distress God seeth not, God succoureth not; his hand cannot reach, his mercy cannot save. Now mark what the prophet Esaias saith, to such a perplexed soul: 'Why sayest thou, my way is hid from the Lord?' 'No, no, my sins are greater than can be forgiven,' saith the despairing soul. Then, methinks Satan is stronger to overthrow thee, than God to save thee. Then it seemeth sin is stronger to condemn thee, than God to do good unto thee. Thus you make God to be weaker than sin, than hell, than the devil. And this is most injurious to God.—And what can you say more, and what can you do more, against the Lord?"

"This sin of desperation, as it is most injurious to God, so it is extraordinary dangerous to thy own soul. It is that which taketh up the bridge, and cutteth off all passages; and there can no spiritual comfort and consolation come into the poor soul of a sinner. This despair of the soul is that which cutteth the sinews of all man's comfort, and taketh off the power and edge of all means of grace. It daunteth all a man's endeavours; nay it plucketh up a man's endeavours as it were quite by the roots. For that which a man despaireth of he will never labour after. 'Alas,' saith a man, 'what skilleth for a man to pray? What profiteth a man to read? What benefit in all the means of grace? The stone is rolled upon me, and my condemnation sealed for ever. It is sure in heaven, and therefore I will never look after Christ, grace and salvation any more. The time of grace is past, the day is gone.' If christians would pray for him, and ministers would labor to do him good, he biddeth them spare their labor, for hell is his portion, and his condemnation is sealed in heaven. See now and consider what desperate danger despair bringeth to a poor heart; and maketh him to be beyond the reach of mercy, that no means can come at him."

The following passages are like many others in which Mr. Hooker explains the way of a sinner's relief, both from the burden of his guilt, and from the despairing tendencies of which he may be the subject. "The gospel alone reveals that which may satisfy our spiritual necessities and answer the expectation of our faith and the desires of our souls, upon the sense and feeling of those evils, which, as insupportable, would otherwise sink them. This is the argument the apostle gives, Rom. 1 : 16, 'I am not ashamed of the gospel of Christ; for it is the power of God unto salvation.' And why? 'For therein is the righteousness of God revealed from faith to faith,' that is, from one degree of faith unto another.

"A man is unrighteous, and possessed of the power and presence of it, and under the hand of revenging justice, by reason of the same. And where may a righteousness be found, which may answer the necessities of the soul? The law never discovered this. The creatures never heard of it. The wisdom of man could never reach it. Nay, the excellency of all the knowledge of all angels was never able to devise it. But Christ, who came out of the bosom of the Father, hath wrought this righteousness, and by the gospel hath 'brought life and immortality to light,' (2 Tim. 1 : 10,) which otherwise had never seen light. And therefore it is that the glad tidings of peace is said to come this way, and is not to be heard from any other coast. Tidings of evil come, like Job's messengers, from every quarter. Tidings we hear from the law are nothing but threatenings and wrath, ready to condemn us. Tidings from our own hearts are nothing but guilt and fear to terrify and arrest us. Tidings from hell are yet worse, there be nothing but accusations subtil and malicious; and those present us at home and abroad, in earth and in heaven, at God's tribunal, and require present execution to be done upon such undeserving creatures. Only glad tidings come from the gospel. '*This is a faithful saying and worthy of all acceptation, that Jesus Christ came into the world to save sinners.*' And therefore the soul looks out and says, 'It may be.' This keeps the head above water."

From the passages which have thus far been given, we see with what fidelity he deals with the conscience of the man unregenerate. This class of extracts may properly be closed with one more, applicable to the condition of souls effectually called to Christ.

"Now that which I conclude withal, is this: you see how far the Lord hath brought us; how the soul hath been prepared, and cut off from sin and himself, if fitted for the Lord Jesus by contrition and humiliation, and that the soul comes to see that there is no hope in creatures, nor any succour in heaven but the Lord Jesus Christ. And so, at last the sinner comes and lies at the foot-stool of the Lord Jesus Christ; and knows that either he must be another man, or a damned man. Now he sees that prayer and all other means will not profit; and the power of the means yet prevail not; and the power of his corruptions is not yet mastered. Then he looks up to Christ; and is contented that he shall do what he will with him.

"Now, when the Lord Jesus Christ sees him lie wearied thus with his corruptions, then the Lord gives special notice to his soul, that it is his purpose to do him good, and there is mercy for that broken heart of his. With that, hope is stirred, and saith, 'Is it possible? Is it credible? Shall all this wretchedness of mine be pardoned?' Desire is kindled and longs for that day; 'O that I might once see the funeral of my sins!' And then love and joy are cheered to entertain this mercy; and say, 'O how is the soul bound to the God that offers free and undeserved grace to a stubborn rebellious-hearted sinner!' At last the will saith 'Amen,' to the promise, and saith, 'O, that mercy I will have.'

"Thus the soul is come home to God by vocation. Now the prodigal is come home to his father; and the father's heart leaps within his breast when he sees him lie at the door. And, as the Father rejoiceth, so the Angels in heaven rejoice. And all the faithful should rejoice, and say, 'O my husband,' or 'my father,' or 'my child is come home again;' and 'my wife that was a sinful woman is come home again to her first and best husband.' You that have found it thus in yourselves, be comforted. You that know it in others, rejoice. Thus we have heard how the soul is ingrafted into the stock of Christ."

From the foregoing selections, and from numerous others which might be given from various parts of his works, illustrative of Mr. Hooker's manner of instructing the unconverted, it is to be seen that he was accustomed to throw his whole soul into the concerns of the sinner in his unregeneracy; to feel in a most lively manner for him as guilty, and as exposed to "the righteous judgment of God," and to the woes of "the second death." And then, too, he enters with great earnestness into the subject of his rescue; the possibility of it, the way and means of it, as set forth in "the glorious gospel of the blessed God," with the purpose of helping the sinner to understand the way of relief and how to avail himself of it. In short, as an instructor of those in an unregenerate state, he illustrated that beautifully simple idea of Cecil, respecting a faithful minister, "*A sinner trying to help a sinner.*" He seems to have had in vivid and tender recollection his own experience as a sinner, before he came into the peace which is through a crucified Jesus, "remembering his own afflictions, the wormwood and the gall." And his may properly be regarded as an instructive example of deep ministerial sympathy in the miseries of the sinner as "having no hope, and without God in the world,"—as "far off," and yet to be "made nigh by the blood of Christ."

In his instructions to the regenerate, Mr. Hooker's writings give evidence that having, as already remarked, studied the christian in almost every conceivable variety of spiritual state, he knew how to bring from the treasuries of divine instruction whatever was adapted to his necessities. He had no sympathy with the views of those who seem to think that it is a matter of course for a christian to move on faithfully, happily, safely and prosperously towards heaven. He appears to have viewed the christian as one who was to be watched with unceasing care, by the under shepherd of Christ's flock, as to be counseled, cautioned, sometimes rebuked; and many times to be helped as in spiritual trouble; and, as exposed to countless moral and spiritual vicissitudes, to be the object of unceasing sympathy and prayer, by the watchman for souls.

A few extracts from his works, illustrative of the foregoing remarks, may be classified as they relate to the christian's duties, his enjoyments, his spiritual trials and perplexities, his temptations, conflicts, encouragements, and final certainty of blessedness.

THE CHRISTIAN DUTIES. These, of every kind, he was accustomed to press, with great earnestness and fidelity; whether they respect the divine honor, the good of men, or the christian's own advancement in the divine life.

*Wherein lies the great strength of the christian to do his duties.* "Thou that art one of Christ's, here is thy comfort; whatsoever God in his word biddeth thee to do, he, by his promise hath undertaken to make thee able to perform. Truth it is, the things that God hath commanded thee to do, they are wonderful hard, even impossible to flesh and blood; but yet, notwithstanding, to thee easy and possible, because God hath undertaken to give thee strength to do them. So that thou hast great cause to be encouraged, considering the power of God. The power of God is with thee. It is bound to be thine, by his promise; and if God be able thou shalt obey whatever he hath commanded thee, *so thou wilt believe this promise, and use the means."

*Faith necessary to the energy of obedience.* "When the father of the possessed child, (Mark 9,) brought his son to Christ to be cured, 'Lord (said he,) if thou canst do any thing, have compassion on us and help us.' If thou canst do it? saith Christ; 'If thou canst believe, all things are possible to him that believeth.' So I say to such of you as are willing to obey God's commandments in all things, are you able to believe this doctrine that I have this day preached? that God will make you able, upon your endeavours to do all he commandeth? If you could believe this, all obedi-

* If, or on condition that.

ence were possible. But here is thy fault, (if it be not in the former,) thou canst not believe that God will give thee strength over every lust; a lust that is strong in thee by constitution, is strong in thee by custom, by education; a lust that hath so great a rooting in thee; that hath so often foiled thee; that God will help thee against such a lust. Because thou canst not believe, here is the cause thou canst not obey God's commands. What a shame is this, for thee not to believe the God of truth; not to be able to take his word; when his word is confirmed by his promise; when his promise is seconded with his oath; when his oath is accompanied with so many seals, as thou hast received every time thou hast received the Sacrament of the Supper; and yet, notwithstanding, thou art not able to believe; what a shame is this!"

*Conformity to Christ.* "Did not Christ give the least improvement of heart to any sin? not practice the least sin, in any measure? Then go thou and do likewise. Be thou like thy Saviour, that thou mayest have some evidence that thou hast a title unto him. 'Have no fellowship with the unfruitful works of darkness, but rather reprove them;' 'be ye followers of God as dear children.' Christ had no sin, nor fellowship with sin. Let his course and practice be thy copy.

"But some will say, 'Would you have us to be saints, here on earth? How can it be, that we should know no sin, when we have such a body of death hanging upon us?' Yes, we may know no sin, though it do hang about us. The apostle does not say, *equal* God in holiness, but *imitate* him; and he doth not say, follow him fully, but even '*as dear children*.' The Father is infinitely full of holiness. Follow God 'as dear children;' do what you can; and then cry to him to enable you to do what you cannot do. It was the practice of David, (Psalm 119: 4, 5,) 'Thou hast commanded us to keep thy precepts diligently; O that my ways were directed to keep thy statutes!' As if he had said, 'I know the Law requireth it, and it is my duty to do it. Help, Lord; and take, Lord; and carry, Lord, thy poor servant, and lead me into the land of righteousness.' It is an evidence of one that is born of God."

*How to form a right judgment of thyself.* 1. "Thou must first repair to the word, and thereunto attend daily. So look into the uprightness and sincerity of thine own soul, which may in some measure answer the word. Hear what the word will say, and see what work of grace is in thy heart, that will answer the word. And join sides in the testimony of the happiness of thy condition. Be sure to take thy soul at the best. Do not always consider what is the worst in thee, and go no farther. Do not only see thy failings and infirmities, on the one side, that accuse thee. But see if there be any soundness and uprightness; any goodness and truth of heart that may speak for thee. Hear both sides. It is injustice to hear one side, and determine the cause thereby. As the Lord deals with his servants, so shouldst thou deal with thyself."

2. "Labour to have thy conscience settled, and convictingly established of that truth, of that grace, which reason now informed doth entertain, and the word doth witness to be in thee. Mark, I say, if there be any want of assurance of God's love, and settling thereof to thy soul, so that evidence of the work of grace doth not come powerfully in upon thy heart; but there is some guilt of sin remaining, and conscience still begins to accuse thee, and condemn thee. The truth is, though reason be informed; yet, haply conscience will breed new broils at every turn, and put in new pleas, and so nip, disquiet, and torment our hearts, in staggering our hearts. Therefore, as we must have our judgments in-

formed out of the word, that there is some good and soundness in our souls; so we must get conscience persuaded of it; that conscience may be on our side, and speak for us."

3. "We should strive mightily to have our hearts overpowered with the evidence of the truth, which reason and conscience make good to us; that it may quietly entertain it, and humbly and calmly welcome it; that to what reason saith, and conscience concludes, the heart may say, Amen; and set its seal to that, and yield and subject itself to it."

4. "Maintain the truth, which upon these good grounds thou hast received, and thy judgment and conscience and heart has submitted unto. It is the cunning of the enemy to lead you out; and he will have his vagary, and this turning, and the other wavering; but keep to the point; be sure to hold to that truth that hath established you, by the evidence of reason, and testimony of conscience, and the evidence of your souls. Let me teach you a little, that are weak;

"*How the soul being tempted, may answer Satan's accusations.* Satan, when a man hath got a little the advantage, he will begin to play the lawyer.

"*Satan.* What, dost thou not yet see what

wants thou hast, and how many failings; how unfit for service, and how weak for service?

"*Poor Soul.* It is true; but it is written (Prov. 28: 13,) He that confesseth and forsaketh his sins shall find mercy. Though I be weak, and feeble, and unfit, yet I confess and forsake my sins; therefore I shall find mercy.

"*Satan.* Aye, that you do indeed. Doest thou not apprehend, and doth not thy conscience witness, that thy heart is averse, and untoward to duty, and unwilling to come thereunto, weary therein, and desirous to be free therefrom?

"*Poor Soul.* (Keep to the point and answer.) I have many sins and many failings, it is true. But yet it is true, he that confesseth and forsaketh shall find mercy. But I confess, and forsake; therefore I shall find mercy.

"*Satan.* Aye, but are you tampering with God's privy counsel? Do you know to whom mercy belongs? Secret things belong to God; he must give his mercy to whom he please, and his goodness to whom he sees fit.

"*Poor Soul.* (Keep still to the point, and say,) I know not what God's secret will is; but I know what the word saith, and what the Lord saith, and what conscience saith. I know, I confess, and forsake; therefore I shall find mercy.

"*Satan.* But many cozen themselves; mercy is a rare gift; few have it; and many dream of it, that shall never share therein or partake thereof, and why may not you be one of these?

"*Poor Soul.* (Keep still to the point, and answer.) It is true, I may cozen myself; and my heart may be deceived. But the Lord will not cozen me; and the word cannot deceive me; and the Lord and the word say, he that confesseth and forsaketh shall find mercy. But I confess and forsake; therefore I shall find mercy.

"*Satan.* How do you know that you do apply the word aright? May you not be deceived in that? The word is true and certain, but how do you know that you do fitly apply this word?

"*Poor Soul.* I know it not but by the word; and I repair thither that I may know it. And the Lord knows all; and the word informs me that whosoever confesseth and forsaketh his sins shall find mercy. And my conscience knows that I do confess and forsake; therefore I shall find mercy. And, Satan, if you will show me any other text contrary to this, I will yield; but otherwise I will never yield, while the world stands.

"Thus you see how you may hold Satan to the word and keep him there. But if he lead you into wildernesses, and by-paths; and take you to fears and suspicions, you are gone. Ps. 119: 98, 'Thou through thy commandments hath made me wiser than mine enemies.' "

*The sufferings of Christ an appeal for christian fidelity.* "Hath our Saviour thus suffered; and hath he stepped in between the wrath of God the Father, and the faithful?* Justice saith, 'that soul hath sinned, and must be damned;' and anger saith, 'I must break out against that soul.' Then the Lord Jesus Christ steps in and saith, 'I will bear all, and undertake the satisfying of all; I will bear all those punishments due unto him.' You that are believers and have a share in Christ, unto you I speak. Labor thou, from hence, to see the heinousness of sin; and to hate it because it hath brought all this evil upon thy Saviour; and would have brought the same upon thee, had not the Lord Jesus Christ stepped in between thee and the wrath of the Father: Oh, look what thy sin hath done unto the Lord Jesus Christ; and see if you can love it, and take contentment in the commission of it. Let me teach you how to do it. Send your thoughts afar off, and see our Saviour in the garden, cry-

* i. e., The believer.—Ed.

ing out and saying, 'My soul is exceeding sorrowful, even unto death,' 'watch and pray;' and also when he was in bitter agony, and 'he prayed more earnestly, and his sweat was as it were great drops of blood falling down to the ground,' and his soul was almost broken within him, under the fierce indignation of the Lord; and he fell upon the ground; and yet all this would not do the deed. Follow him to the cross, and see him attended with the soldiers, and pierced through with a spear. See then if thou canst love thy sins which have done all this. And farther,—listen a while and hear that cry, 'My God! my God! why hast thou forsaken me?' Have you the hearts of men? I don't say of Christians. Oh brethren! it went very heavy with our Saviour. O go your ways home. I charge you in the name of Jesus Christ, and answer your own hearts, or rather, answer the petitions of our Saviour, and say, 'Lord, why hast thou forsaken? Oh Lord, it was for my pride, and my contempt of thy word, and my despising of holy duties, and for the rest of my sins I should have been forsaken; and thou wast contented to be forsaken for me.' Oh, can you consider this, and love your sins still, which have brought all this misery upon the Saviour? I charge you brethren, as ever you had any tender love unto Jesus Christ, or any regard of your own comfort, go your ways, and be forever cast down and humbled for those evil ways of yours which brought our Saviour to such a gulph of misery; and to be angry with those sins which made God the Father angry with the Lord Jesus Christ; and take thou revenge upon that proud and stubborn heart that brought all this misery upon thy Saviour."

*The sense of sin, under the life of righteousness.* "They that have the life of righteousness in them; they do in their hearts apprehend sin to be the greatest evil, and the most bitter thing that is in the world, whether it be a great sin or a small sin, in regard of the matter of it; whether it be a secret sin, or a public sin, in the circumstances. However sin may differ, yet they apprehend the greatest evil and bitterness to be in all sin,—you have Paul for this; Ro. 7: 24, 'O wretched man that I am, who shall deliver me from the body of this death!' The remembrance of that original corruption that was in his soul, and could never be rooted out, this made him cry out for deliverance."

*Growth in knowledge of our own vileness.* "Grow every day up in the observance of thine own baseness, and in the acquaintance of thine own weakness in the best of thy duties. This is a sweet pitch of a christian; the more God bestows and the more grace God vouchsafes, he goeth his way and hangs down his head, and wonders at God's goodness, that ever the Lord should help a poor creature so to call upon his name; and says, 'Lord, it is thy grace; it came from the assistance of thy spirit.' But that ever a wretch should say to his services and duties, 'ye are my gods;' abhor this in thy soul; and keep a marvellous dislike of thyself, and a low esteem of thy duties; and be wondering at God's grace; and admiring at God's mercy; and return to God that hath given thee power to perform any service; and lie thou in the dust; and trample on thine own performances. Do as Paul did, 'But what things were gain to me, those I counted loss for Christ." (Phil. 3: 7.)

*The slow but sure death of sin.* "For howsoever Christ doth not kill 'the old man' presently; yet he killeth it certainly. And when once the death-wound is given, it can never be recovered again. Hereby you may try whether there be a death of sin in you; however you may find in yourselves all the parts and kinds of sin and corruption, the several lusts and inclinations of the flesh rising and bubbling up in you; however, sometimes, particular corruptions may have a very strong hand, and put forth abundance of might in you, to the mastering and captivating of you, so that you are for the present 'sold under sin,' as the apostle Paul speaks of himself, Ro. 7 ; yet, if there be this weakening of corruption, and that universally and constantly, it is most certain there is a death of sin in you."

"*How you may know the life of righteousness.* Wherever there is a life of righteousness, there is a seeking after God and the things of God ;—God in himself, God for himself, God as he is accomplished with his holy excellencies, and admirable attributes and perfections. As he seeks after God ; so he seeks after the things of God ; the favor and mercy of God ; the presence and fellowship of God ; those glorious inheritances which are God's and are called God's and because they are with him. The things of the kingdom of God, they are the things he seeks after, that hath the life of righteousness in him."

"Where the life of righteousness is, there is a suitableness of the spirit and agreement of the heart to the whole law of God. I beseech you observe this ; the body of righteousness is nothing else but as it were the stamp of God's law ; there is a proportion and conformity between one and the other. Therefore, in whomsoever the life of righteousness is in his spirit, there is a suitableness of disposition to the whole law of God. So that howsoever there is much antipathy, and deformity, and unlikeness, and disagreement from the law of God; yet, notwithstanding, there is something within that soul, that is agreeable to the whole law of God. So that there is no particular part of the commandment of God, but it doth find a principle to which it is suited and agreeable, in the heart of all those that have the life of righteousness in them. And this, I take it, is the meaning of that writing of the law of God in their hearts; that is, the very law of God in all the parts of it. It hath a stamp and impression, and a resemblance in the spirit of all them that have the life of righteousness in them."

"Wherever there is the life of righteousness, there are all the fruits of the Spirit, in some part and in some measure, begun in them. The life of righteousness is not the springing up of one grace, but it is the quickening of the whole body of grace in us. The whole frame of holiness is begun in them that have the life of righteousness. There are all the fruits of the Spirit to be found in that soul. Take the lowest and meanest christian of all others; if he have the life of righteousness, he can find in himself (if he do not judge falsely,) at least the buddings and blossomings of 'the fruits of the spirit' of God; of that which God requireth of his children. And it is lasting, never dying life. When this life of righteousness is quickened and begun in any, it increaseth and groweth up, it never dieth or is finally extinguished."

The works of Mr. Hooker abound in passages like the foregoing, giving delineations of the various duties of the christian life. He begins with the heart, as the first and great scene of duty, where there is to be continually going forward the performance of the works of holiness, in the certainty that that christian who is faithful in the secrecies of his soul as under the eye of a holy God, will be faithful in the duties of the visible life.

With the same particularity with which he delineates the christian's duties, does he likewise show HIS PRIVILEGES. These means of nourishing the plants of grace in the soul, he highly prized. Of the many examples of this class of instructions to the regenerate, a few only can be given here.

*Timely storing up of the divine promises.*—"I would have a good christian store up all the good promises of God, in all the good word of

God, seasonably; I mean when all thy parts and abilities are strong, and nature is able to fight it out, and while the fair day of God's favor lasteth; and while the word and sacraments are dispensed. This is the best time to lay in the promises of God, that we may not want [lack] them when we have use for them. We must lay in promises of all kinds. It is the wisdom of a man to have somewhat to spare, and to have an overplus before-hand; that a man may not live feebly and poorly, and be at his wit's end at every turn, and knows not which way to shift for himself and have no bread in his house; I mean no provision of promises by him."

"*How to live by faith.*—The Lord brought thy unfaithful heart to believe: now labour to husband this grace well; to improve it for thy best good, and live by it. It is a marvellous great shame to see those that are born to fair means,—I mean the poor saints of God, that have a right and title to grace and Christ,—and yet to live at such an under-rate. I would have you to live above the world. Though thou hast not a coat to cover thee, nor a house to put thy head in, yet, if thou hast faith, thou art a rich man. It is a shame, I say, to see them that cannot husband that happy estate which they have. They live as if they had it not; so full of want, so full of care and pride, so weak, and unable to master their sins; whereas, the fault is not in the power of faith, nor in the promise, nor in the Lord; for the Lord doth not grudge his people of comfort, but would have them live cheerfully, and have strong consolations, and mighty assurance of God's love. 'Rejoice in the Lord alway, and again I say rejoice.' God hath sworn 'that by two immutable things, wherein it is impossible for God to lie, we might have strong consolation, who have fled for refuge to lay hold on the hope set before us.' We do the Lord and his promises a great deal of wrong, and bring an ill report upon that grace and mercy of his, when we open the mouths of the wicked, and make them say, 'Oh, these precise people talk of quiet, and contentment, and joy in the Holy Ghost; there is great talking of these things, but we could never see it yet.' Oh, brethren, are the riches and revenues of faith so great, that a christian may live like a man all his days? Let all the drunkards and malicious wretches against God laugh and be merry; yet they cannot see one of those days that a poor saint can, though he should lie in prison all his days."

"*How to make faith limber and quick.* First

we must maintain the evidence of this grace once gotten, without question, undeniable, without controulment,—I say, faith once gotten. This must be the care of every man; he must know the nature of faith in general, and of his faith in particular; whether his faith be of the right stamp, and will stand him instead, in the day of account; and whether it be that faith of which Peter speaks, (for there is a great deal of copper* faith in the world.) When thou hast gained evidence that thou hast faith, then fill it up, and keep it by thee, and labor to have the demonstration of this work so plain in thy soul, that it may be past denial. Go to God, and to his word, and to thine own soul, and to the ministers of God's word; and advise wisely and judiciously of thine estate; and labor to see sound evidences of the work of grace in thy soul; and see them every day, and read them every morning, noon and evening, and get them by thee, and learn them; that when thou comest to improve thy faith, thou mayest not question whether thou hast it or not. And if thou wilt not be persuaded, yet look to the promise. But if thy doubting comes still upon thee, and controversy still oppresseth thee, and is set on foot

* Counterfeit, spurious.—Ed.

against thee, then reason thus with thine own soul: 'If I have *not* faith nor grace, I am sure I shall never get it by looking upon mine own corruptions and distempers. Where must I have it, if I want it? The promise only must do it.' Therefore look you to that. It is with a doubting man as with a man that is melancholy. If he would but set upon the work, he would see his own folly; and by going he would be able to go; and by speaking he would be able to speak. So this vain dismayedness of heart, and these discouragements of a doubting soul, do more hinder the work of faith than any distemper else. Therefore, when thy fears and discouragements come in upon thee, go thou to the promise, and in going thou wilt be able to go.

"When thou hast thus maintained the clearness of the work of grace before gained, then labor to bring your heart to a marvellous stillness and calmness from time to time, that you may give way to faith, and that faith may have its full scope to frame thy heart. Stayedness and stillness of soul frames the heart to hold the shield [of faith] steadily, and bear the blow comfortably, when it comes. Those boisterous affections, those crowds and troops of troublesome imaginations, as fear and jealousy and superstition; these do unrank the frame of the soul, that it cannot command faith. When it was told the disciples that Christ was risen from the dead and had manifested himself to them, the text saith, 'They believed not, for joy, and wondered.' As it is true of immoderate affection, so it is true of strange fear, and care, and distemper; because they hurry the soul so violently, and transport the soul that he cannot believe. So it is with a soul troubled with tumultuous thoughts, especially melancholy; and those enemies, of vain imaginations of fears, and sorrow, and distempered thoughts and cares; that though the heart is willing and able to believe, yet those stirrings of boisterous affections, they cross faith in the way, and bear down faith, that it cannot go on in the way of promise towards God, nor receive help from him. David chides his own heart, Ps. 43 : 5, and rocks it asleep, and would bring it quiet, saying, 'Why art thou cast down, O my soul, and why art thou disquieted within me? Hope thou in God, for I shall yet praise him who is the health of my countenance and my God.'"

Selections might be multiplied to a great extent, illustrative of Mr. Hooker's peculiarly felicitous manner of setting forth the privileges of the children of God, and the methods by which to maintain their consolations and joys, in the divine life. That ministry is, in one of the best points, a ministry to the edification of the church, which promotes, in an evangelical manner, and on solid, scriptural grounds, the happiness of christians in all their privileges.

THE CHRISTIAN'S TRIALS. — To this subject, as entering largely into the experience of the children of God, Mr. Hooker, in his writings, has devoted attention to a greater extent than almost any christian writer whose works are extant. Passages concerning these, as they stand related to the various subjects which he discusses, appear in every part of his writings. The conviction comes upon the reader, at almost every step, that the writer himself must have had extensive and unusually deep experience of them, and must have been an accurate and constant student of them, as they appear to the observing minister in his intercourse with christians around him. Such graphic delineations as he gives of the christian's trials, in their various nature and forms, could be given only by one who had himself "endured a great fight of afflictions." It is a circumstance which imparts great value to Mr. Hooker's writings, that he evidently so well understands and appreciates the necessities of the children of God, as arising from uncounted and endlessly diversified forms of spiritual affliction. And by his wise, discriminating, and faithful counsels, he seems to have aimed to prepare the christian for any exigency of the divine life which might arise. The comparative infrequency with which such subjects are treated, in religious writings in recent years, will justify the quotation of passages from Mr. Hooker's writings, under the present classification, somewhat extensively.

*Advice to a soul "pestered with vain thoughts."* "Imagine thine heart begins to be pestered with vain thoughts, or with a proud or haughty spirit, or some base lusts and privy haunts of heart; how would you be rid of them? Why you must not set up and pull down, and set up and pull down, quarrel, and contend, and be discouraged. No, but eye the promise, and hold fast thereupon, and say, 'Lord, thou hast promised all grace unto thy servants; therefore take this heart, and take this mind, and take these affections; and let thy Spirit frame them aright, according to thine own good will. By that Spirit of wisdom, Lord, inform me. By that Spirit of sanctification, Lord, cleanse me from all my corruptions. By that Spirit of grace, Lord, quicken and enable me to discharge every holy service.' Thus carry thyself and convey thyself by the power of the Spirit of the Lord; and thou shalt find thine heart strengthened and succoured by the virtue thereof, upon all occasions. The text, Rom. 8: 2, saith, 'The law of the Spirit of life in Christ Jesus, hath made me free from the law of sin and death.'"

"*How we may get help against the stubbornness of our own hearts.* Do not tug with this resistance, in thine own power, or any ability that is in thee; do not in thine own strength contest with that rebellion, for it is certain this will make it excessive rebellious. When thou seemest to offer violence to thyself, thou wilt be more cross; nay, thou wilt grow to a kind of fellness and fierceness of opposition against the work of God's grace. Sin becomes out of measure sinful, by the commandment, Rom. 7: 13, and instead of quarrelling with thy sins, thou wilt quarrel with the Almighty, saying,—'If I do what I can, why should not God help me?'"

"You will say,—'*What shall I do?*' Come and bring thy soul into God's presence; lay thy self down in his sight; and tell the Lord, that thou art a traitor; and which is worse, thou canst not but be so; that is thy misery. Make known all the base abominations of thy heart and life before the Lord, and all that crossness and opposition that thou findest in thy soul to Christ and his grace. Beseech him to take away the treachery and falseness of thy heart. Beseech him that he would do that for thee which thou canst not do for thyself. Tell him that thou wouldst chuse *not to be,* rather than to be thus treacherous. Tell him that he hath said he 'will take away the heart of stone,' Eze. 36 : 26 ; and that it is not in thy power to put it away ; and, therefore, leave thy soul there, beseeching him to make known himself as a God hearing prayers, pardoning sins, and subduing iniquities. Plead the covenant of grace, and the promises of it, that all is freely, and firstly, and wholly from himself; that he must *make us his people*—he must make us humble and broken-hearted. Look to Jesus Christ, and beseech Him that 'hath the keys of hell and of death,' that he would unlock those brazen gates and doors of thy heart."

"Do not fear the terror of the truth, so as to step aside from under it, and withdraw thyself from the stroke of it; but think of the goodness of it. As a man, though he fear the bitterness of the pill, yet knowing it is a means of his health, he is willing to take it. So here; when God moves, move thou; when He stirs, stir thou. Many a man neglects the stirrings of the Spirit of God, and never hath the like again; and then on his death-bed cries for his old terrors. Oh, therefore when the truth meets you and stirs you, keep the heart under it, and follow the blow in secret; and bless God that hath opened thine eye, and affected thine heart in any measure; and let thy heart lie still, under the stroke of the truth. Possess thyself with the criticalness and danger of that condition thou art in. 'In regard to the secrecy and difficulty of the work, how easily may I be deceived; and how dangerous if it be.' A failure here can never be repaired afterward. If never broken *for* sin, then never broken *from* sin; then never united to Christ; and then thou never shalt see the face of God in glory. Think how many have miscarried in this place. As when the mariner sees the mast of a ship, he fathoms the water and tacks about, and looks about him, 'lest,' says he, '*we* split upon the rocks also.' So do thou look to thyself here. Thousands have sunk and split themselves here, and thou art in danger. And know that if thou dost miscarry here, thou art undone for ever."

*Reasonings with a sin-seeing and distressed soul.* "In Christ are all the treasures of all mercy and all compassion, of all grace and salvation; whatever is needful for us and may be beneficial to those that believe in him, and rest upon him in a true and lively faith. And however the soul may think this treasure may be spent, and this fountain of compassion and mercy drawn dry, and says—'can my sins be pardoned? and my corruptions subdued?'—Christ doth prevent this also. We may spend what we will; there is still enough to spend upon, Ep. 3 : 8. There are *unsearchable riches in Christ.* As who should say,—'Thou knowest no end, thou findest no bottom of the vileness of thy heart, that doth pollute thee and defile thee; there is no end of the riches of Christ, no bottom of the ocean-sea of God's mercy that may comfort thee and relieve thee upon all occasions. Christ received the Spirit above measure,' John 3 : 34. As if Christ would prevent the cavils of a poor creature, and pluck up a discouraged heart. When the sinner thinks,—'my sins are out of measure sinful, and my heart is out of measure hard;' why think and remember that in Christ there is mercy out of measure merciful, and grace out of measure powerful."

*Satan's temptations to the Christian to despair.* "A desperate kind of despair and discouragement sometimes oppresseth the soul of the distressed sinner. The soul looks upon his own corruptions, and unworthiness and sinfulness; and then he dares not come to Christ. He views the number of his sins so many; the nature of his abominations so heinous; the continuance of them so long; the soul of a distressed man sends his thoughts afar off, and views all, both the abominations of his life and the distempers of his soul, and seeth his iniquities mustering up themselves. And Satan helps him forward; for this is his policy. First he will keep a sinner that he shall not see sin, and then all will be whole, and the sinner thinks,—'there is mercy enough in the Saviour, and why should I trouble myself.' But when Satan sees the sinner will pore upon his sins; then, he shall see nothing else but sin; so that he dares not go to God for mercy. Now, tell the sinner that is in this case, that mercy is in Christ, and redemption offered in a Saviour, he dares not hear of it, he dares not think of it. 'What,' saith he, 'shall I once think or imagine that there is any mercy for me? that I have any title to, or interest in Christ? that were strange.' And the soul is here foiled and fastened upon his own misery, and never goeth to the Physician. He stares into the wound, and never goes to the Saviour. For a man is as well kept from going to Christ by poring continually upon his distempers by despair, as by resting upon his own sufficiency by presumption. This is the course of Satan, and herein he is marvellous cunning."

"But this should not be any discouragement to our hearts from coming to the Lord Jesus Christ. For whom did Christ come into the world? For whom did Christ die? When he came, it was not for 'the righteous;' they needed him not; but for the sinners that had condemned themselves. He came to save those that could not save themselves. 'This is a faithful saying, and worthy of all acceptation, that Christ Jesus came into the world to save sinners, of whom I am chief.' There is a fountain set open for all people to wash in; all sorts of sins, and all sorts of sinners. Be they what they will be; be they what they can be, their sins never so great, the time never so long, and the heinousness never so vile, come; they that will come; come and welcome."

"*Why God has left sin in the hearts of his saints on earth.* It is but to serve you; as the Canaanites that were left in Canaan. They shall not reign over you, saith God. They shall be tributaries to you. I speak this to your comfort only, that are the Lord's. You are priests to God the Father, and you must have sacrifices to offer up unto God. Whenever thou mortifiest a sin, it is as pleasing a sacrifice to God as if thou offerest up an ox or a sheep. Thy sins do more to further thy grace than any thing else. They help thee to draw the water of godly sorrow, of true repentance. They help thee to prize the mercies of the Lord Jesus Christ; they help thee to humility, to meekness, to a spirit of compassion to others. Be of good comfort therefore; if thy sins be grieved for, striven against, laboured against, they further thy reward for all eternity. Be exhorted therefore to fight against your sins. Thou that art one of Christ's, what cause can be better than thine; the cause of Christ against the Devil? What greater assurance can there be of obtaining the victory; seeing God himself is engaged in the quarrell. The word is gone out of his mouth, 'for sin shall not have dominion over thee.' Oh then, stand it out against sin. Never yield the bucklers to thy corruptions that make hard upon thee. Make the battle fresh and strong against thy lusts. Though thou art foiled again and again, never give over conflicting; for God hath said it, and his word shall never fall to the ground, 'sin shall not have dominion over thee.' He hath engaged, himself, in the cause; and if

God be true, and able to keep sin from reigning over thee, thou shalt be sure to have the victory, in the end, fall on thy side."

" *The workings of a soul under saving godly sorrow.* The heart is most of all weary of the burden of sin *as it is sin;* and thinks it the greatest burthen in the world. As a man that hath a great burden on his back, wrincheth this way, and that way; and if he cannot remove it, yet he will ease it; so the heart useth all means, and taketh all courses, that if it were possible it may cast off and ease itself of the vileness of sin, and plague of sin. This wearisomeness of soul, which followeth the weight of sin, makes itself known thus:—his eye is ever upon it; his mouth is ever speaking of it; and he is always complaining against it; and he is readily content to take shame to himself for it. He will never meddle with, nor give way to any thing that is sinful. The soul will not dare to tamper with any thing sinful. Why? because it hath been wearied with the burden of it before. When the soul seeth sin as it is sin, and that it is a burden to the soul, and the heart is now weary of it; it will lay no more weight upon it, because now the heart is weary enough already. If a man hath been once at death's door, by drinking deadly poison, he will never taste it more. Nay, he will not endure the sight of that cup; he will rather fare hardly, and rather starve, than eat and drink that which shall kill him. 'So,' (saith the soul,) 'it is sin that hath made a separation between me and my God;—had been the death of me, if God had not been merciful to me; and therefore I will rather sink and die, than meddle with these sins any more.'"

*Reproof to religious despondency.* "This doctrine, 'Ye are not under the law, but under grace,' affordeth sharp reprehension to all such as are the children of God, and find themselves to be so, by a testimony from their own spirits and from God's Spirit; and yet, notwithstanding, lead lives uncomfortable and lumpish.—Thou art in Christ; and yet art thou discouraged or disheartened, either with corruption or with guilt? How unworthy dost thou walk, of that condition wherein thou art. Thou art 'not under the law, but under grace;' why then is it, that thou art as much dejected and discouraged as if thou wert 'under *the law*,' and *not* 'under grace.' What is it that makes thee disconsolate and discouraged, but the condition wherein thou art may administer to thee much more comfort? Art thou full of sin? Yet, notwithstanding, thou art in a condition wherein all sin shall be pardoned. Is thy obedience very imperfect? Yet thou art in a condition wherein imperfect obedience shall be accepted, and frailties covered. Dost thou find that God commandeth thee much, and thou doest but little? Yet, thou art in a condition wherein the Lord hath promised, (so thou wilt use the means, and trust upon him,) to make thee able in an acceptable manner to do all that he biddeth thee do. Doth the law threaten? Doth the law curse? Yet thou art in a condition wherein neither the threatening, nor curse of the law, shall ever reach thee, to condemnation. Findest thou mighty rebellions in thy nature, against the law of God? Yet thou art in a condition wherein is promised a new nature, which shall be conformable, and subjected to the law of God.

"What should make thee, therefore, hang down thy head? Sharply are such Christians to be reproved, that, being 'in Christ,' lead lives as if they were out of Christ. Dost not thou make the world think that that is false which Christ saith, 'for my yoke is easy and my burden is light?' 'If Christ's yoke is easy and his burden is light,' why is it, (saith the world,) that the servants of Christ walk so disconsolately, and complain of heavy burdens?

"Indeed, I do not deny but it becometh christians to mourn;—and they that do not mourn, shall not rejoice in the day of judgment. And the people of God are '*mourners in Zion.*' Yet, what kind of mourning? There is a double sorrow; a 'godly sorrow,' and a 'worldly sorrow.' A godly sorrow is when a soul melteth into tears, upon the consideration of his sins and wants, because he believeth that God, through Christ, will accept him, notwithstanding them all. This sorrow, the more of it the better. This sorrow melloweth the heart; softeneth the heart; makes it frameable to the impressions of the word of God. But now the other sorrow, which is a worldly sorrow, when a soul is beaten out of heart because of sin formerly committed, because of mighty corruptions that do annoy him, to mourn without hope and confidence of acceptance; this is worldly sorrow, and causeth death; this is altogether unbeseeming christians. Receive now this sharp reprehension, and be humbled for it, and labour to remember your condition. '*Ye are not come to mount Sinai, but to mount Zion;*' '*Ye are not under the law, but under grace.*' Therefore, '*rejoice in the Lord, always;*' and be so cheerful that the world may see that the service of Christ is a sweet service."

While Mr. Hooker, thus, and in numerous

other portions of his writings, exerts himself very skillfully, and with great kindness and fidelity, to meet and relieve the spiritual troubles of true christians ; he still makes most thorough and searching work, in dealing with the consciences of christians for their sins. He leaves no proper means untried to help them to see how their *sins* have brought on their perplexities ; for example :

" When the saints fall into some gross sin, or else are at truce with some bosom corruption, though but an infirmity ; then God doth withdraw his presence. For obedience is the term of God's presence. 2 Chron. 15: 1. 'He is with us while we are with him.' If, then, the saints break company, no marvel though Christ withdraw his society. John 19: 21. This is the tenure of Christ's manifestation, provided we love him. But if not, he is gone. Ps. 51. 'Create a new spirit within me,' as who should say, all is to begin anew. This God doth to show his indignation against sin. He will not bear nor bolster it ; no, not in his own. And this God doth, not only when they sin foully, but when they are at truce with a distemper, though but an infirmity. As for example, if a christian be overtaken ordinarily with a choleric distemper ; if a christian be eager of the world, or grows dead in services; it is just with God that these men should be destitute of their comforts."

While Mr. Hooker thus treated of the duties of the christian, and of his trials; and dealt with his conscience and his fears, in relation to his short-comings or sins; he was also accustomed to set before him the ENCOURAGEMENTS derivable from "the good word of God." His pages abound with passages, rich in instruction and ministrations to the good courage of the true christian, on such topics as the following: The cause of the christian against sin, the cause of Christ; Encouragement to the burdened with sin; God's faithfulness dispensing his fatherly love to his children; Strong and invincible consolation from all the faithful performances of the Lord; The believer to be one with the holy and blessed God; Christ able to resist and vanquish, when his people cannot; The happiness of our being in heaven, to behold the glory of the Lord Jesus Christ; Our union and communion with Christ, "the top of our happiness in heaven." Such topics as these he unfolds, illustrates, and applies, for the encouragement of the true child of God, in such fullness, clearness, sweetness, as is excellently fitted both to make him joyful, and at the same time humble, that with such "strong consolations," he yet lives so far below his proper standard of both christian fidelity and enjoyment.

While many of the passages which have been quoted from the writings of Mr. Hooker, suggest the inference, that he had himself deep and various experience as a christian; numerous others might be given which show that he had such experience in no ordinary degree. His heart as the seat of such experiences, is evidently, and fully in his trains of thought and remark, on such topics as the following: The free and full confession of sin by the contrite; Sorrow for sin makes us set a high value upon Christ; The effect of brokenness of heart upon our views of this world; The vileness of sinful thoughts; How a contrite sinner prizes and covets deliverance from sin; Faith waiting on the will of God; The feelings of those rightly affected under a faithful ministry, towards those who exercise a faithful ministry; and numerous other experimental topics.

The attentive reader of his writings will meet with a great many passages which indicate the closeness and care with which he was accustomed to study the unrenewed heart, in its ever varying workings, against the truth and the Spirit of God. He exposes also, with a masterly hand, the cavils and objections and subterfuges, by which men in an unregenerate state set themselves against the proposals of the gospel to the guilty, and the requirements of duty on the conscience. He drives the sinner from one refuge after another, with skill, fidelity, seriousness, urgency ; and yet with a manifest kindness and warmth of desire to see him flying to the refuge provided at the foot of " the cross." He never *wrangles* with the unregenerate man ; but he bears down upon him, in that union of solemnity and love to his soul, which in the pulpit must have often overwhelmed his hearers.

The writings of this skillful instructor show him to have been very critically discriminating and accurate in his whole treatment of the great subject of *evidences of grace ;* and that he was accustomed to set in very clear contrast with each other, the genuine and the spurious, in religious profession. Illustrations of this statement might be given, in passages from his works on such points for discrimination as the following : The difference between the outwardly reformed, and the inwardly renewed ; The different ways in which godly and worldly sorrow drive men ; The difference between true and false confessions of sin ; Selfish and evangelical sorrow for sin compared; The two operations of sorrow for sin, and hatred of sin; The way for an unrenewed man to know what is his taste; False means for curing sorrow for sin; The difference between the weight of sin, seen simply as a subject for punishment, and seen as an infinite evil before God; The skill of the hypocrite in deceiving men, even the ministers of the gospel; The treacherous hypocrite; The complaining hypocrite; The discouraged hypocrite; The lazy hypocrite; The judicious, but self-deceived professor; The terrified hypocrite; The uselessness of the christian ministry to hypocrites.

There occur frequently, in the writings of Mr. Hooker, passages which relate to the christian ministry; especially the manner in which its duties are to be conducted; which explain the peculiar characteristics of his own methods of preaching. Such passages are found, sometimes in the form of fraternal counsels and exhortations to his brethren; sometimes in the forms of explanation to hearers generally, of the proper principles for the exercise of the ministry. Some of his topics of this class are the following:—Ministerial self-application of preaching; Ministerial cultivation of faith; How a powerful ministry is evinced; The utter powerlessness of the ministry, without the accompanying influences of the Holy Spirit; Description of a pointless ministry; and A "needle-headed ministry";* The fault of generalizing, in preaching; How to carry ourselves towards those who are wounded for their sins; The fearful import of God's word, in its applications to sinners, as it effects the heart of the minister; How to know a faithful minister; and numerous other like topics. A minister entertaining such views as Mr. Hooker cherished, on such subjects as these; acting upon them, with the fidelity in which he appears to have acted; and, by weight of talent and elevation of christian character such as his, qualified to act by his influence on the minds of his brethren in the sacred office, must have been of inestimable worth to both the ministry and the churches of his time. Would that he might live again, in the influence of his works, upon our own and yet coming generations!

Next to the grace of God, abundantly imparted to this Father in the ranks of the Puritans, as explaining the reasons of his peculiar excellence and success in the sacred office; we place the

* "Needle-headed men who are sharp and eagle-sighted in search of secrets," &c.

fact that he PREACHED THE BIBLE. He could have preached philosophy, had there been occasion for it; and brought forth abundance from the treasures of science and learning, with which he was familiar, and knew how to use in their proper place. But he adhered to that apostolic injunction, "PREACH THE WORD." He seems to have written every sermon, and sentence of a sermon, with his Bible *open* beside him; and to have traced every line of truth by the light shining from its holy pages. He makes great use of the language of Scripture in his sermons. His explanations and expositions of the meaning of Scripture are those of both the scholar and the devout christian. When he has unfolded the meaning of his text, he employs it as a spiritual magnet, to attract together multitudes of other Scripture passages belonging to the subject in hand; and so sets them all along in his discourse that they make his path of thought and reasoning to shine. His unfoldings of Scripture thought are natural, simple, clear, and often beautiful.

In his methods of illustration and exemplification, he is appropriate and skillful. He draws most for these, from the facts of Scripture history, and from the developments of human nature in society and the world at large. It strikes us as remarkable, that with all his learning, there is scarce a classical allusion to be found in all his pages of pulpit matter; or a fact of any kind employed, which might be out of the circle of the reading and knowledge of his hearers. His aim appears to have been to be *understood*, so that his preaching might be *felt*. And from all that appears in the history of his preaching, by cotemporaries and others, he secured that object effectually. Sometimes, it is true, his illustrations are quaint and quaintly expressed. He has also the peculiarity of the old writers of his time and of some more recent, that his illustrations of the various workings of depravity and impenitence are drawn from certain scenes, and certain vices and forms of profligacy and irreligion, which the taste and habits of our own times do not often bring into notice in the pulpits of our own country. And the decent, and respectable, and moral, and intelligent sinners of many a New England congregation, might think such illustrations, used now, to be helpful in keeping the truth from disturbing their consciences, inasmuch as they are not vicious and profligate and shameless in their visible life. But for the purposes which he had in view, under the circumstances of his ministry, as exercised in England, especially, and probably in Holland, even such illustrations must have carried with them great force.

The style of Mr. Hooker's writings, regarded as being substantially that of his pulpit discourses, has the prime excellencies sought by all men whose aim is to instruct and reach the conscience and the heart. He appears to think of little else, in his use of language, but to employ words which, with the least possible impediment, shall carry his thoughts into the minds of his hearers. Rarely is he diffuse. And in general there is a terseness and force in his methods of expression well worthy of the study and the imitation of the young preacher. With the description of his manner of pulpit delivery, quoted in a former chapter, before our minds; and reading his discourses, so simple in style, so scriptural, so rich in thought and forcible in description and illustration; and keeping in mind as to be associated with these, his deep and strong feelings, and his fervent devotion; it is no mystery that he was followed, venerated, and loved, as an eloquent and powerful preacher of "the gospel of Christ." As was said of a more recent and effective preacher, might it with equal truth be said of Thomas Hooker, "whoever saw him in the pulpit, saw a man in earnest."

In the application of his subjects to the minds of his hearers, Mr. Hooker had the habits of the Puritan preachers of his time; of dividing the concluding portions of his discourses into *Uses;* with this difference, that he gave himself a much wider range in the terms he employed in their statement. Among his discourses will be found, variously distributed, such as the following: "Use of Instruction;" "Use of Comfort;" "Use of Direction;" "Use of Exhortation;" "Use of Reprehension;" "Use of Reproof;" "Use of Terror;" "Use of Examination;" "Matter of Wonderment;" "Use of Admiration;" "Use of Thankfulness;" "Use of Trial;" "Use of Assurance;" "Use of Patience;" "Use of Humiliation." His remarkable skill in thus applying truth to his hearers, led one of his brethren to say of him, that "he was the best at an *Use*, of any preacher he ever knew." While these methods of concluding discourses have, to modern tastes, an appearance of art and stiffness; still as we read on in the writings of Hooker, and perceive what powerful *Uses* he makes of his subjects; there is such a richness in the matter, such skill in its application for its legitimate purposes; such closeness, solemnity, adaptedness to reach and move the inmost feelings of the heart; that the peculiarity of the term

*Use* is forgotten; and we find ourselves occupied with the work which the preacher is doing with his subject, upon the minds of his hearers.

## CHAPTER VIII.

Different writers on Congregational Church Polity. Results of their discussions. Hooker's "Survey of the Summe of Church Discipline." Spirit as a controversial writer.

It was a natural consequence of the secession of our Puritan ancestors from the established church, that both in England and in this country they should early have taken up Ecclesiastical Polity, as a subject for earnest inquiry. Their love to the Scriptures as the great depository of divine instruction, naturally led them to "search the Scriptures," daily, that they might learn thence what is the Constitution of the Church of Christ. With all the respect they felt for the established Church of England, in consideration of the things good and right which there were in it, and of their former membership of it; and with all their reverence for the good men who remained in it and in the ranks of Conformity; they acted, still, upon that great principle taught by the Lord Jesus Christ, "*And call no man master upon earth; for one is your Master, even Christ; and all ye are brethren.*"

That different men, among the New England Fathers, should have written books, setting forth the results of their inquiries, was to be expected. It was their privilege, and their duty. And liberty to write, teach and publish their views on this great subject, must have been one of their sources of enjoyment, as time passed on with them, in this land of peace and religious freedom. We find their works on Church Polity, therefore, in such number, and of such ability, as to assure us that the Puritan Fathers were no idlers; nor disposed to spare study, research, pains, and labor, in discussing a subject of such magnitude, and so deeply involving their liberty of conscience, their order, comfort and spiritual prosperity. They did not discuss this subject so much for their brethren yet residing in England, as for themselves. The good fathers and brethren in England could take care of the interests of the subject for themselves. The New England churches and ministers had their own wants to provide for, as laying foundations for a new community of the followers of Christ, and for a nation which was to be born.

In the catalogues of the various writings of the Chief Fathers of New England, we find numerous books on Congregational Church Polity.

Among them were Cotton's Keys of the Kingdom of Heaven; Cotton's Way of the Churches; and that Way Cleared; also his Holiness of Church Members, proving that visible saints are the matter of the church; Davenport's Powers of Congregational Churches; Samuel Mather's Apology for the Liberties of the Churches of New England; Discourse concerning Baptism and the Consociation of Churches; the Powers of the Pastor in administering the Sacraments; A Dissertation concerning the right of the Sacraments; Answer of the Elders of the New England Churches, to Nine Positions; Answer of the same to Thirty-two Questions,—both these last attributed to Richard Mather; also his Answer to Herle, in Defence of the Way of Congregational Church Government; New England Brethren's Ratio Disciplinæ; and Thomas Shepard's Discourse, tending to clear up the Old Way of Christ in the Churches of New England.

Besides these books by good men in New England, the great interests of Congregational Church Polity were promoted in England by John Owen's Enquiry into the Original, Nature, Institution, Power, Order and Communion of Evangelical Churches; Dr. William Ames'

Fresh Suit against Ceremonies; Bartlet's Model of the Church Way; and others.

These strong men, on both sides of the Atlantic, were not likely to make any half-way work, of discussing a subject which had such hold on their hearts, and so involved their rights, and called for the outlay of their powers. There was every thing in their circumstances to drive them to their Bibles and to their closets, in their search for light. Especially moving them to such resorts, was the preciousness of the privileges they sought, and the value of which privileges they had learned in the old country, and in the severe school of ecclesiastical oppression and persecution. If ever christian men were certain to evolve and settle great first principles, to state them justly, and defend them ably and courageously, these were the men.

Nor were they doing a work which should turn to account for the future interests of Congregationalism alone, in this country. They were discussing and settling great principles which were to be for the use and benefit of other denominations of christians, to have existence in this country; who were to live under our republican form of government; and who should deem it their privilege to exist, and to enjoy their rights as christians and as men, without being amenable to Episcopal authority, or being dependent for their privileges in the word and ordinances of the New Testament upon the ministrations of Episcopal hands.

One remark farther; the principles of Congregationalism, thus early discussed, and thus ably and earnestly defended and brought into contact with New England mind, both in and out of the churches, were, in truth, the principles,—derived from the word of God itself,—which were to come into use for the good of the free State, as well as for the free Churches. The *republicanism* of the Bible pervaded the writings of those devoted men, on Church Polity. The grand elements of our national Constitution and Government were found by them, in their studies of this subject; and they brought them forth to the acceptance of the men of the civil State; and those elements came into powerful action in the country, long before the arrival of that great crisis, the American Revolution. They appeared in the Declaration of Independence, and have been embodied in our national and State Constitutions. These general remarks will be found illustrated, while we proceed to give some account of Mr. Hooker's "Survey of the Summe of Church Discipline."

A brief history of this book is here appropriate, and will be given as contained in the prefatory Epistle to the Reader, signed by Edward Hopkins and William Goodwin, brethren in the church of which Mr. Hooker was pastor, in Hartford, and dated October 28, 1647: "The present discourse was finished by himself, in the time of his life, and sent, near two years since, to be made public; but the Lord, in whose hands all our works and ways are, determined otherwise. That sad Providence was entertained by him in reference to the present work, with much contentedness and humble submission to the good pleasure of the Most High; and if he might have enjoyed the liberty of his own judgment and desires, no farther discoveries should have been made to the world of these his labours, and they would have been buried in everlasting silence. But at last he was overborne, and condescended to what now is again advanced; though before the full transcribing, he was translated from us, to 'be forever with the Lord.' The reader may well conceive, had the judicious author lived to peruse the copy now sent, the work would have been more complete, and perhaps some additions made in some parts thereof. But we have not yet had the happiness to find among his papers what was intended of that kind."

"The sad Providence," to which allusion is made in the preceding extract, was, the loss of the ship in which the book was first sent, with all the voyagers. "The first fair and full copy of this book was drowned on its passage to England; with many serious and eminent christians, which were buried (by shipwreck) in the ocean." The reflection, by his friend Rev. Thomas Goodwin, of England, in his Introduction, is here added: "The destiny which hath attended this book hath visited my thoughts with an apprehension of something like omen to the cause itself; that after the overwhelming of it with a flood of obloquies and disadvantages, and misrepresentations and injurious representations and injurious oppressions cast out after it; it might, in the time which 'God hath put in his own power,' be again emergent." "I have looked for this, that this truth and all that should be said of it, was ordained as of Christ, of whom every truth is a ray, to be as seed corn; which, 'unless it fall into the ground and die,' and this perhaps with some of the persons that profess it, it brings not forth much fruit."

His own opinion of the book is here given also, by Rev. Mr. Goodwin, who superintended its publication in England: "As touching this treatise, and the worthy author of it, I intend not to preface any thing by commendation of either unto the reader; which were indeed to lay paint upon burnished marble, or add light to the sun."

The full title of the book in question is as follows: "A Survey of the Summe of Church Discipline. Wherein the Way of the Churches of New England is warranted out of the word, and all Exceptions of weight, which are made against it, answered; Whereby also it will appear to the Judicious Reader, that something more must be said, than yet hath been, before their Principles can be shaken, or they should be unsettled in their practice. By Tho. Hooker, late Pastor of the Church at Hartford upon Connecticott in N. E. Isa. 62: 1. For Zion's sake I will not hold my tongue; and for Jerusalem's sake I will not rest; untill the righteousnesse thereof break forth as the light, and the salvation thereof as a burning lamp. 1 Cor. 13: 8. For we can do nothing against the truth, but for the truth."

This work was printed in London, in 1648. Like nearly all the other works of the author, it has never had a republication in this country, and is now very rarely to be found. Its importance among our early works on the subject, and it not having been reprinted for more than two hundred years, will justify a particular description.

Mr. Hooker defines Ecclesiastical Polity to be "a skill of ordering the affairs of Christ's House, according to his word." The positions which he maintains, given as near as practicable in his own language, are as follows:

That Christ is the Head of the Church, by his spiritual influence, and by his special guidance in the means and dispensation of his ordinances:

That the Church is composed of believers, professing the Christian Faith, and by voluntary consent and covenant yielding subjection to that government of Christ which he has prescribed in his word:

That the government of the Church comprises the dispensation, by its proper officers, of preaching, prayer, seals and censures, and the conduct of the affairs of the Church generally, according to the provisions and rules of God's word:

That the institution of the Church issues from the special appointment of God the Father through the Lord Jesus Christ as head thereof, by the Holy Ghost sent and working to that end:

That visible saints only are fit matter appointed by God to compose a visible Church of Christ; the judgment respecting who are such, to be made up in the judicious exercise of christian charity:

That that which gives constitution and being to a visible Church is the mutual covenanting and confederating of the saints, in the fellowship of the faith, according to the order of the gospel:

That profession is the public manifestation of our assent to the doctrine of faith, as in word delivered and received by us; and our resolution to persist in the maintenance of the same:

That the Church of visible saints, confederating together to walk in the fellowship of the Faith, being thus the essence or substance of the Church, is before all officers:

That in the New Testament, Churches Congregational, only, are of Christ's appointment and institution:

That Ecclesiastical Power, under the scripture name of "the keys of the kingdom of heaven," is supreme and monarchical as it resides in Christ; and is subordinate and delegated, as it is a right given by commission from Christ to fit persons, to act in his house according to his order; this last being in the many when combined, or in one, when it is given to him by the election of the many:

That the government of the Church, in regard of the people, is Democratical; in regard of the elders or rulers chosen by the people, Aristocratical; in regard of Christ alone and truly, Monarchical:

That to the ministry and guides of the visible Church the Lord Jesus has committed "the keys;" i. e. the power delegated from himself to dispense and administer the holy things of his house, according to his will prescribing the order:

That a Council of Churches is an assembly of Pastors, and of Delegates or Commissioners, duly qualified in christian character, gifts and knowledge:

That Church Communion implies community among christians in receiving and enjoying the ordinances of Christ dispensed by his ministers:

That for the offices of the Church there is required a visible company of christians who must concur and consent to call tried and approved persons, to bear office among them; consisting of Pastors, Teachers, and Ruling Elders; these instituted by election and ordination, and having their prescribed duties:

That a Bishop, or Episcopus, is three-fold;

either 1. *Divinus*, as, by divine institution and according to the word of Christ, "set in the Church:" or 2. *Humanus*, as by consent of the assembled Pastors and Delegates called to preside or moderate in their sessions: or 3. *Satanicus;* such an Episcopus as the enemy Satan, acting the pride and suiting the sovereignty of the spirits of men, hath, by a mysterious way, successively and secretly brought into the Church; that so he might midwife Antichrist into the world; and while the Pope, as universal Bishop, is "the Man of Sin," the Bishop, especially when he has mounted into the Arch-bishop's chair, is *the Child of sin*, or "the Man of Sin" in his childhood; appropriating to himself to be sole Rector, Pastor, and Judge:

That the duty of officers in the Church is, to bestow their whole man, and their whole strength, and study, upon their weighty and worthy work; receiving their maintenance from the provisions of the Church to that end:

That the office of Deacon is, to husband the estate and temporals of the Church; faithfully to keep, prudently to dispense and dispose it to such uses and persons as shall be required by the Church; to provide elements for the Lord's table, and to provide for the poor, and to dispense whatever the Church put into his hands for " him that ministers: "

That ordination is an adjunct to election, consequent and consummating; and is the solemn introduction of a minister, already elected, into the free exercise of the functions of his office; approving and solemnly confirming him in his office, by prayer and the laying on of hands:

That the dispensing of ordination appertains to the teaching Elders, under authority of "the presbytery: "

That the term *Independent*, in its fair and inoffensive sense, imports that every particular Church, rightly constituted and completed, hath sufficiency in itself to exercise all the ordinances of Christ:

That the work which is of common concernment to the members of the Church, when not convened, is that watch which they stand engaged to express to each other for the good of the body so confederate:

That the members of the same Church have special power over one another, by virtue of their covenant; and in case of offences by brethren, we have express law from Christ, by which we are bound to pursue unto conviction, and are also charged to prevent and to seek the removal of all taint of sin:

That in the examination and admission of members, the rule according to which satisfaction is to be regulated concerning their qualifications, is on this wise; if a person live not in the commission of any known sin, nor in the neglect of any known duty, and can give a reason of his hope towards God; this is cause, with judicious charity, to hope and believe there is something of God and grace in the soul, and therefore fitness for Church society:

That in the reception of members from other Churches, on their recommendation, the testimony of any Church of Christ ought to be accepted according to the worth of it, and received with all the respect due to the spouse of Christ:

That they who have right to administer the sacraments, are those called thereunto by God's command, and the allowance and designation of the Church; viz. Pastors and Teachers; and they who have right, by rule and allowance of Christ to receive the sacraments, are those who have come to ripeness of years, and are rightly received, and stand members of the visible Church:

That the children of those who are members of the Church are to be baptized:

That the sacraments must be dispensed publicly, in the presence and with the concurrence of the Church solemnly assembled:

That Baptism is the sacrament of our institution and engrafting into Christ:

That the Lord's Supper is the sacrament of our nourishment and our growing up in the Lord Jesus; and therefore is appointed by him to be frequently used:

That the Lord Jesus Christ has appointed Church censures, to purge out that which is evil; and that herein the members of the same Church proceed not only christianly, but judicially, against offences:

That offences are either private, as known to one or more; or public, as famous and notorious in practice:

That where we have not found ground for conviction, we have no reason to administer an admonition:

That excommunication, being an ordinance of so great terror, must be proceeded in with much moderation, pity, patience, and long-suffering; must not be hasty, nor for small aberrations, but for evils which are either heinous or abominable:

That the highest tribunal where the sentence of excommunication issues, consists of the fraternity or brotherhood of the Church:

That the sentence issued, is to be solemnly passed and pronounced upon the delinquent, by the ruling Elder; whether it be the sentence of admonition or of excommunication:

That the consociation of Churches is not only lawful but very useful; keeping in mind, nevertheless, that they are of limited power; that their judgments are to be regulated by the rules of Christ, from whom comes their power; and that their authority, designed by Christ, is the authority of Church counsel; rather than the authority of Church jurisdiction, as by some is held:

That a Synod is a meeting ecclesiastical, by communication and combination; consisting of fit persons, called by the Churches and sent as their messengers, to discover and determine of doubtful cases, either in doctrine or practice, according to truth; and having power to set down their judgments clearly and definitively; not tc leave the Churches whence they are sent, in doubts and demurs; they dogmatize their sentences, and set down their determinations as sure truths, to their judgments and apprehensions; and so return them to the Churches whence they came; and their determinations take place, not because they concluded so, but because the Churches approved of what they have determined; but they have not power to inflict censures, nor to impose their canons or conclusions upon the Churches.

It is proper here to notice and correct an error which appears in Hanbury's "Historical Memorials,"* relative to the authorship of the "Survey of the Summe of Church Discipline," of which an account has now been given. Mr. Hanbury states that it is the joint work of Hooker and Cotton; and gives the title of the volume on which he has founded his opinion. A copy of the same book in the Library of the Old South Church, Boston, is found to be neither more nor less than Hooker's "Survey," and Cotton's "Way of the Churches Cleared;" bound together between the same covers, with a general title page adapted to the united contents of the volume; but, the two works themselves bearing all the evidences, internal and external, of separate authorship, which ever appear in the cases of any books written by different men.

Unfortunately for Mr. Cotton, as well as Mr. Hooker, Mr. Hanbury, while he devotes between fifty and sixty pages to an account of what he entitles "Hooker's and Cotton's Sur-

* Published under the auspices of the Congregational Union of England and Wales.

vey," yet closes his chapters on the book without any account of Cotton's "Way of the Churches Cleared." It is to be hoped that in future editions of the "Historical Memorials," justice will be done to these New England Fathers, by the correction of the error respecting the joint authorship of "the Survey," and by the addition of a fair account of Cotton's "Way of the Churches Cleared." "Honor to whom honor is due."*

This being the only work in which Mr. Hooker appears as a controversial writer; it is here in place to remark on his character and habits in the conduct of a religious controversy.

His candor is eminently manifest. Of his principal opponent, Rev. Samuel Rutherford, Professor of Divinity in the University of St. Andrews, in Scotland, he observes, in his preface, "Among those worthies whose pens and pains the Lord has been pleased to improve, Mr. Rutherford hath deserved much for his indefatigable diligence; a man of eminent abilities; the depth of whose judgment, and sharpness in dispute, is evidenced beyond all excep-

* The above statement indicates to the reader the source of the mistake relative to the authorship of the "Survey," which appears in the Life of Mr. Cotton, vol. I, p. 259, of this series.

tion, by that accurate and elaborate piece of his Apologetical Exercitations, wherein he appears to be *Malleus Jesuitarum*, and their factours and followers, the Armenians, who receive their errors by wholesale from them and retail them out again in their particular treatises. And for these pains of his I suppose the Churches will, (I must profess, for mine own particular, I do,) owe him much. And therefore it was a pleasant providence, when I perceived by some books put forth of late, that he did address himself seriously to debate of Church Discipline; a subject, as of special difficulty, so of special advantage to the truth, and of help to the present times in which we live."

Of Mr. Hudson also, from whose views on the subject of a "Church Catholick Visible," Mr. Hooker felt constrained to dissent, he yet says, "Master Hudson is a learned man, and a faithful minister of the gospel. When I had considered his writing, twice and thrice, I found his judgment sharp and scholastical, his spirit christian and moderate, his expression succinct and pregnantly plain to express his own apprehensions. So that my heart was much contented with the acumen and judicious diligence of the author. Though I could not consent to what he writ, yet I could not but unfeignedly prize the learning, perspicuity and painfulness expressed in his writing."

Mr. Hooker's spirit appears kind and courteous, even while carrying forward the most masterly refutations of the positions of his opponents. He is at the utmost remove from any thing proud and overbearing. He makes good, throughout his book, that which he says in his preface: "In handling all these particulars, so full of difficulty and obscurity, I am not such a stranger at home but that I am easily sensible of the weight of the matter, and of mine own weakness; and therefore I can profess in a word of truth, that against mine own inclination and affection, I was haled by importunity to this so hard a task, to kindle my rush candle, to join with the light of others; at least to occasion them to set up their lamps."

He most conscientiously aimed not to misunderstand his opponent, and thus become liable to do him injustice. On one of Mr. Rutherford's passages he frankly says: "When I had read over Mr. R. once and again, I was at a stand in my own thoughts, to determine certainly what was his proper intendment. I profess in a word of truth, I would not willingly misconceive his meaning, and so wrong him and the truth."

Mr. Hooker is sometimes most amusingly playful and adroit,—when his opponent has incautiously weakened his own position by something he has written,—in making him answer himself. His skill in overturning the positions and arguments of an opponent is masterly and irresistible. He was too well trained as a logician, and too well accustomed to the discriminating and critical examination of questionable doctrines advanced, however ingeniously or plausibly stated, to render it safe for an incautious or unskillful reasoner to fall into his hands.

In the review of the discussions of Mr. Hooker as they were designed to controvert the sentiments of Professor Rutherford, it is natural to make the reflection, that the differences between good men here on earth, which do not involve the fundamental articles of the christian faith and practice, need be no bar to their christian fellowship on earth; nor can they embarrass their final union as members of the church triumphant in heaven. Rutherford, as he appears in his experimental and practical writings, was a man of deep, serious, ardent, heavenly-spirited piety; one with whom Hooker, as a devout christian, could not fail to feel a strong and lively sympathy. He is believed to be the same of whom the Rev. Richard Cecil, in his Remains, says: "Rutherford's Letters is one of my classics. Were truth the beam [of the scales,] I have no doubt that if Homer, Virgil, and Horace, and all that the world has agreed to idolize, were weighed against that book, they would be lighter than vanity. He is a real original. There are in his letters some inexpressibly forcible and arresting remonstrances with unconverted men."*

And Rutherford, when he came to reply to Hooker in his "Survey of the Survey," thus expresses his regard for his character: "As I intend to darken the reputation of no man; so far less to undervalue the authority and name of the servant of the Lord Jesus Christ, *Mr. Thomas Hooker*. Yea, the commandment of God lays laws upon me, to give testimony to his learning, his dexterous eloquence and accuracy in disputes; and as christian report bears, to judge him one who walked with God and preached Christ, 'not with the enticing words of man's wisdom, but in demonstration of the Spirit and of power.'"

Mr. Hooker's Survey, as already remarked, appears to have been a more extended work

* Cecil's works, vol. III, p. 347.

than some of the others on the same subject, in his time; and was highly valued among the New England churches, as a digest of the elementary principles of Congregationalism. It has been stated, in a sketch of his life several years since given in a periodical work, that "from his opinions was digested the Platform of 1648."* It may have been used, as were the works of Cotton, Shepard, and others, for such a purpose.

The principles of Congregational Church Polity, however, as in practice in New England, and so widely extending their influence over our western country at the present day, were not brought forward by any one man; nor were they matured as the act of the good men of any single period in our New England history. To have perfected such a system is an honor which belongs to no one man, nor to the fathers of one generation. The minds, hearts, and hands of many good and great men, guided by "the Spirit of the Lord," and who have written at different periods, and added to the stock of instruction, have been concerned in this thing. The present matured condition of Con-

* Conn. Evang. Magazine, I, 445. See also Cong. Ch. Order, edit. 1845, p. 24.

gregational Church Polity in New England is the fruit of the experience, prayerful study, and careful discussions of the good men of two hundred years; and of the previous period of the progress of Puritan principles in the father-land. It was not to be expected that any single writer, of all the New England Fathers, let his talents have been what they might, would embody all which could be needful in one digest for the government of the churches. No one man's book would be adopted, unanimously, as containing all which was necessary, and having nothing to which exceptions would be made. Nothing more therefore is claimed, or can properly be claimed, for Hooker, or Cotton, or Davenport, or Shepard, or any other man, than that "he hath done what he could" to assist in settling the great first principles of Congregationalism; humbly and confidently leaving the work to be carried forward by following generations of wise and good men, according as experience and farther study of the subject should make progress. All that is claimed for the subject of this memoir, therefore, is simply that which has been said by a distinguished writer on Congregational Polity, of our own time and country: "The venerable wisdom of John Cotton, and the logical acuteness of Mr. Hooker, of

Hartford, stood side by side and shoulder to shoulder with the learning of Robinson and Owen, not to mention many other renowned names; and had a share in forming the goodly proportions of our Ecclesiastical Structure."*

* Upham's Ratio. Disciplinæ, p. 32.

# CHAPTER IX.

The posterity of good men a subject for inquiry. Hereditary merit disclaimed. The Scripture method of treatment of the subject of posterity. The descendants of Mr. Hooker viewed in their different professions and stations in the church and in the country, and their relations to general society. Concluding reflections.

In a country like New England, peopled to a considerable extent at first by Puritans, the lapse of more than two centuries has rendered it natural to inquire respecting their descendants. Especially is this an inquiry of some interest, relative to the posterity of men who bore a prominent part in the formation of its fundamental institutions, civil, political, and religious. Their residence, number, character, positions in the church, in the state, and in relation to the literature, professions, morals, and benevolent enterprises of the country; and also to its interests agricultural, commercial, financial, manufacturing, &c.—all these are points for inquiry. And last, though not least, we naturally wish to learn how, in the more retired, domestic, and social relationships of life, they have been concerned in giving character to general society.

For, after all that may be said relative to the public or professional worth and eminence of individuals, the fundamental elements of good and happiness in the civil state, are found in its domestic and social circles, in the homes of its families, and in the characters of those who fill those homes. If there be not moral and intellectual worth there, it exists nowhere. If it does exist there, it is sure to find its way into the fabric of the state.

Thomas Hooker came to New England, that he with his associates then, and their posterity after them, might first of all worship God according to the dictates of their own consciences; and next, that they might enjoy that civil liberty which is the proper associate of religious freedom. He did not seek these ends in vain, as we have seen in former chapters. He assisted in laying the foundations upon which the New England States especially and their churches, have been built up; and by which, in confederacy with the other states in our Union, they have labored to found and confirm this republic. Every faithful historian of our country recognizes and most fully declares what Winthrop, Haynes, Cotton, Hooker, Eaton, Davenport, and their associates accomplished, in furtherance of the religious order, civil stability, social happiness, and prosperity which have been so richly enjoyed.

While, however, this subject of inquiry is considered, and while its results may show, in the case of any given worthy or father of New England, that his descendants have sustained, in good measure, his reputation, an utter disclaimer is here entered against the doctrine of hereditary merit, in all its branches. Men are worthy of respect, not because the blood of good and worthy ancestors runs in their veins, whether those ancestors were in the high walks of society in a republican country, or in the ranks of royalty or nobility, in a kingdom or empire. They are worthy of respect, simply and alone, on the ground of their own personal worth.— Men are great in learning and the arts, or by their influence in the concerns of a commonwealth or nation, not through ancestry, but according as they have devoted themselves to study and the acquirement of knowledge, and have employed their talents, attainments, sagacity and experience in promoting the true and best interests of the country of their birth or adoption, and of the world at large. Men are virtuous, not as descendants of the virtuous, but as being themselves the steady and diligent practicers of virtue, and its firm exemplifiers and advocates amidst the tests of virtue to which they are daily called, in such a world as this. And men are christians, not by virtue of a godly parentage and ancestry, but "by the grace of God," and through the active exercise of that grace, in lives of obedience to the divine requirements, as revealed in the sacred Scriptures.

Furthermore, in our contemplations of this subject, we are to be religiously mindful of the instructions upon it, which the God and Father of all men has given us in his word. Without giving the least countenance to pride of ancestry, in any of the human family, the Scriptures give instructions and promises, which encourage fidelity, and confirm the hope of future good and happiness to themselves and theirs, in all those who will rightly receive them, and endeavor to profit by them. Early in the history of the world, God began to speak to man of *his posterity*, as to be the subjects of reward or retribution according to character and conduct in parent and posterity. At the giving of the law upon Sinai, one of the solemn announcements of the divine character and government was: "For I, the Lord thy God, am a jealous

God, visiting the iniquities of the fathers upon the children unto the third and fourth generation of them that hate me; and shewing mercy unto thousands of them that love me and keep my commandments." Every generation of men has had experience of the divine fidelity to this declaration, in fulfilling alike the threatening and the promise thus given. For the encouragement of his people, God has said, "I will establish my covenant between me and thee and thy seed after thee, in their generations, for an everlasting covenant, to be a God to thee and thy seed after thee." The divine condescension has thus been attended with distinct intimations to men, that their choice of good and right ways would take hold on their own good and that of their posterity. "Choose life, that thou and thy seed may live." And as an all-important requisite to holiness, and thence blessedness, for this life and for eternity, God has proffered his own grace, to renew and sanctify: "I will pour my Spirit upon my seed, and my blessing upon thine offspring; and they shall spring up as the grass, and as willows by the water-courses.— One shall say, I am the Lord's; and another shall call himself by the name of Jacob; and another shall subscribe with his hand and surname himself by the name of Israel." The fulfillment of this promise in the gracious renewal and living holiness of multitudes of the descendants of good men, who have lived in all generations, attests the divine faithfulness to this rich and extensive promise.

Join with this promise of divine grace, others which respect temporal good also, and the divine regard to the posterity of the righteous is still farther testified. Instead of the fathers shall be thy children, whom thou mayest make princes in all the earth. Ps. 45: 16. The days of your children shall be multiplied. De. 11: 21. The Lord shall increase you, more and more, you and your children. Ps. 115: 14. The seed of the righteous shall be delivered. Pr. 11: 2. Numerous other promises of temporal good and happiness might be quoted, as embraced in the designs of God toward the posterity of the just.

There is indeed no earthly good, desirable by the children of men, which is not promised to the descendants of the righteous, if found in the paths of the righteous, following their steps, wherein they have been followers of the commandments of God. And to this scriptural and religious view of ancestry and posterity we attach a higher importance and interest than to any view relating simply to the present life, whether as involving honor, wealth, intellectual greatness, length of life, or any of the enjoyments which can be found on this side of eternity, and in the pursuit of sublunary things.

This digression from the historical and biographical track of the present volume, it is trusted will be excused by the reader, as containing the reasons for introducing this chapter. It is proposed to give a brief account of the descendants of Mr. Thomas Hooker, so far as their history and condition in life and society is learned.

Let it here be distinctly noted, that this will not be done as showing, or wishing to show, that there has been any thing peculiar in the case of this man's descendants, beyond those of any other good and great man of his time; nor as placing the posterity of Hooker on higher ground than the descendants of other men of like excellence. A like inquiry into the history of the families of Cotton, Winthrop, Eliot, Shepard, Davenport, and other men of that day, would ascertain like facts illustrative of the subject of worthy ancestry, as followed by a posterity desirous of honoring their descent. And more especially let it here be said, explicitly, that this will not be done to countenance, in the least degree, that family pride which is as contemptible as it is incongruous with the simplicity of republican society. That American, who lays claim to a species of informal nobility of birth and blood, by virtue of his descent from a civil or christian worthy, of other times ; and who affects to look down upon others less favored than himself, with sentiments of disesteem or disrespect, has forgotten, if he ever knew, which be the first principles of republicanism. It may serve to humble this spirit, that from the best and greatest men have sometimes descended some of the worst and basest; and on the other hand, that from men of very humble pretensions and in deep obscurity, have sprung some of the best and greatest men with whom a wise and merciful God has blessed this world. And with our eyes upon these two facts, that Scripture is emphatic, "The Lord of hosts hath purposed it to stain the pride of all glory, and to bring into contempt all the honorable of the earth." "He hath exalted them of low degree." "He raiseth the poor out of the dust, and lifteth the needy out of the dunghill; that he may set him with princes, even with the princes of his people."

Mr. Thomas Hooker had six children, who

lived to ages suitable to enter the marriage relation. The eldest and the youngest were sons. The first, Mr. John Hooker, married in England and resided there, and was a minister in the established church. If he had children, it does not appear that they or theirs ever resided in America. The other son and the daughters, therefore, were the branches of his family from which have sprung the descendants of Mr. Hooker in this country. His first daughter, Joanna, was married to the Rev. Thomas Shepard, the well known and excellent successor of Mr. Hooker at Newtown, now Cambridge, Mass. The second daughter, Mary, was married to Rev. Roger Newton, supposed to have been a student with Mr. Hooker, in preparation for the ministry, first of Farmington, afterwards of Milford, Conn. The third daughter, Sarah, was married to Rev. John Wilson, of Medfield, Mass., a son of the first pastor of the first church in Boston, of the same name. The fourth daughter became a widow, but it is not known whether she had any children.

Mr. Hooker's second son and sixth child was Samuel. He received his education at Harvard University, entered the ministry, and at length became the pastor of the church in Farmington,

Conn. He was a man to whose great worth and excellence Cotton Mather, in his Magnalia, has borne honorable testimony. Farmington appears to have been the residence of more of the descendants of Mr. Thomas Hooker, down to the present time, than any other town in New England.

A catalogue of the descendants of Mr. Hooker, in course of preparation, affords some materials for statements which may interest the reader who has a taste for the study of ancestry. It may be more interesting still, to any who would inquire after their religious character; and their relations to the interests of our country, moral, civil, literary and benevolent.

A little more than 200 years have elapsed since Mr. Thomas Hooker came to New England. The number of generations of his descendants is nine. Of these, a few of the sixth, together with the seventh, eighth, and some young children in the ninth, are now in life. They have resided principally in the States of Connecticut and Massachusetts; although some have resided in New York and Vermont; and others still are scattered in parts of the country farther from the home of their ancestor. Many of them have shared in the spirit of emigration and enterprise, which has led the sons and daughters of New England into distant sections of the country.

They have been distributed in the various professions, offices and employments, in which men render themselves useful to their country; in which reputation, respectability and good maintenance are acquired. The greater part of them have always been Congregationalists; and have held, essentially, the same faith with their godly ancestor, relative to all the evangelical doctrines of the Bible. The relationships which they have formed by marriage have connected them with numerous worthy families; and, in some instances, with lines of descent from others of the early ancestors of New England.

It is worthy of special notice, that a large number of Mr. Hooker's male descendants, forty-two, have been ministers of the gospel; and also that an almost equal number of his female descendants, forty, have been, by marriage, connected with ministers, making a catalogue of eighty-two. These facts are both instructive and interesting, when it is considered that Mr. Hooker himself was devoted to "preaching the unsearchable riches of Christ," as his great and most loved employment. And it also appears, that the number of ministers in the Hooker family, by descent and by marriage, far outnumbers those who are known to have been eminent in any other professions or public employments. The smiles of divine grace have been visibly upon his descendants, in connecting them so intimately with the great interests of the kingdom of Christ; and with the work so dear to his own heart, to which his best talents were consecrated.

Some of these ministers were transferred from pastorships to presidencies or departments of instruction in colleges, or in professional seminaries; some to offices in connection with our institutions of christian benevolence, or to other similar stations of usefulness.*

While such numbers have been connected with the christian ministry, the interests of education, and of the other liberal professions, and of general literature and intelligence, have been served by other descendants of Mr. Hooker, or those who became related to the line of his descendants by marriage.†

* For a catalogue of the ministers, to whom allusion is made, see Appendix, C.

† See Appendix, D.

It cannot be doubted that he desired also that those who should come after him, as his children and "children's children," should serve the commonwealth, the country of their birth and their privileges, as well as the church and the interests of religion. It is a subject for devout gratitude, to Him who appoints to his friends their various fields of service, that it pleased Him to connect so many of Mr. Hooker's descendants, officially, with the public interests of the States of Connecticut and Massachusetts particularly, as well as with those of the country at large; and also that he assigned some of them to the different departments of government, jurisprudence, legislation, and military service in the time of our great revolutionary struggle.* "A man's heart deviseth his way, but the Lord directeth his steps." There are great civil and political interests to be served, in a country like our own; and this, too, by men of high moral character; and, better still, of religious character. Without such services, by such men, the interests of religion itself will be liable to embarrassment and hinderance, if not to entire prostration. When, therefore, God, in his wise

* See Appendix, E.

providence, directs the ways of some of the descendants of his best friends into other professions than the christian ministry, and assigns them the duties and responsibilities of public civil stations; it is, doubtless, done with reference to that great ultimate object, the advancement of his kingdom, in the earth, as "a kingdom of righteousness and peace." Especially may this be regarded as his design, where the descendants of a good man, in considerable number, carry with them the christian character and spirit into their places of trust and office; and discharge their duties there in the fear of God, and from a desire to promote his honor among men. It cannot be doubted that it is of the utmost importance, that into all the departments of human influence and action, in a country like our own, there should be carried the salutary influence of christian principle; as it ensures the virtues of integrity, justice, faithfulness to truth and right. That ancestor is truly honored, whose descendants, wherever they are found, are known as the uncompromising friends and practicers of "whatsoever things are honest, true, just, pure, lovely, and of good report." If there be such a thing as national virtue; or, in better, because Scripture language, "righteousness exalting a nation;" its existence is to be attributed,—next to the grace of God,—to the instrumentality of men, who have carried into the various departments of action and of usefulness, the influence of men in whom dwells "the Spirit of Christ."

To the notices already recorded, of descendants, or of persons related by marriage to descendants of Mr. Hooker, should also be added a considerable number who, for periods shorter or longer, especially in the earlier years of Connecticut and Massachusetts, have been prominent in legislative affairs. In former times, when, without regard to rotation in office, men of experience and sound judgment were elected repeatedly, and perhaps for a series of years, to the different branches of state legislature; men, among the descendants of Mr. Hooker, are found to have served as assistants, or state senators, or as representatives, or in the offices of one or other of these branches of legislature, for successive sessions of from two or three up to more than forty; thus becoming trained to a skill and experience, in public business, which probably contributed much to that wisdom and permanence in the laws, of which notice has been taken in a former chapter.

The genealogical researches respecting the descendants of Mr. Hooker, to which allusion has already been made, so far as pursued, have shown also, that somewhat more than thirty of them have been members of the professions of Medicine and of Law;* a large number have been merchants; several have been bank officers, treasurers to funded institutions, financiers; besides numerous others who have held offices in Congregational or Presbyterian churches, offices of civil magistracy, probate offices, clerkships of courts, sheriffships, &c. In a country, and under a form of government like our own, where the facilities for rising, by usefulness and the force of diligent and faithful discharge of duty, are unembarrassed by hereditary and titled claims; it is the privilege of every man to have employment which shall be honorable; if not in public office, yet, in that estimation in which,—though in the retirement of private life,—an inofficial influence and usefulness gives him a place in the respect, the confidence, and the affections of society.

This volume will be brought to a close, with a reflection on the important consequences

* See Appendix F.

which may result from a single life, of one good man. A great "poet of nature" has said,

> "The evil which men do lives after them,
> The good is oft interred with their bones."

Thanks to the good providence of God, ruling over men, that to the sweeping reflection in the second line of this quotation, there are numerous and happy exceptions. They are found in the cases of the New England Fathers; and in no one of them more clearly, than in that of the good man whose history has been the subject of inquiry. No historian of our country, who has had any respect for the opinions of good men or for his own reputation, has failed to aid in perpetuating their influence by the record of their virtues, and by the history of their acts, in which they have made themselves examples to their posterity. The writings of these Fathers, have in former generations helped on the same important purpose. By both their history and their works, "though dead," they "yet speak."

A very small amount of conscience in an unprincipled writer, may be sufficient to embarress his efforts to perpetuate the influence of a wicked man; and cause him to speak with some reserve, where it is in his power to do great moral injury by his pen. But in writing of such men as the Chief Fathers of New England, self-respect, conscience, common sense, and sound judgment, even where writers do not make a religious profession, all have conspired to urge them to a faithful record of the virtues, by which such men have made themselves blessings to their own time and to uncounted ages following. Thus it comes to pass that a good man is made to live again, for the best interest of his country and of the Church of God; when his mortal life has been long closed. God has appointed that it should be so. And not all the powers of unsanctified intellect, nor of "the Prince of the power of the air, the spirit that now worketh in the children of disobedience," can thwart this purpose of the Divine Mind. The influence of the subject of this memoir is felt in these States to this hour; will be felt, while the religion and the liberty for which the Puritan Fathers struggled, shall continue to live in this nation. To have lived on earth as also did Cotton, Winthrop, Eliot, Shepard, Hopkins, Eaton, Haynes, Davenport, and many others of the ministers and civilians of the time of Hooker; men who "feared God," "eschewed evil," lived in "the faith of Jesus," and died in "the hope of the gospel," and having accomplished for themselves and others the best purposes of this life as preparatory for "the life which is to come;"—to have lived thus is to have lived worthily. To have stamped their own characters upon a youthful nation, so that ages after ages have not effaced, cannot efface, the impressions; and then to have gone up to the rewards of the righteous, to the blissful "inheritance of the saints in light;" this is indeed to have had an existence which is surpassed in excellence and honor by that of but one other order of created intelligencies,—"the angels of God in heaven."

# APPENDIX.

---

## ( A )

*Names of the first Proprietors of Cambridge.*

Jeremy Adams—Matthew Allen—John Benjamin—Jonathan Boswell—Simon Bradstreet, (afterwards Governor of Massachusetts)—John Bridge—Richard Butler—John Clarke—Antony Couldby, (or Colby)—Daniel Dennison—Thomas Dudley, Esq.—Samuel Dudley—Edward Elmer — Richard Goodman — William Goodwin—Garrard Hadden—Stephen Hart—John Haynes, Esq., (afterwards Governor of Connecticut)—Thomas Heate—Rev. Thomas Hooker—Thomas Hosmer—Richard Harlackenden—William Lewis—Richard Lord—John Masters—Abraham Morrill—Hestor Mussey—Simon Oakes—James Olmsted—Capt. Daniel Patrick—John Prat—William Pentrey—Joseph Redinge—Nathaniel Richards—William Spencer — Thomas Spencer — Edward Stebbins—John Steele—George Steele—Rev. Samuel Stone—John Talcott—William Wadsworth—Andrew Warner—Richard Webb—William Westwood—John White.

---

(B)

*Copy of the document accompanying the invitation to Messrs. Hooker, Cotton and Davenport, to the Westminster Assembly of Divines.*

" The expression of the desires of those honorable and worthy personages, of both houses of Parliament, who call and wish the presence of Mr. Cotton, Mr. Hooker and Mr. Davenport, to come over with all possible speed, all or any of them, if all cannot. The condition wherein the state of things in this kingdom doth now stand we suppose you have from the relations of others; whereby you cannot but understand how great need there is of helps of prayer and improvement of all good manners from all parts, for the settling and composing the affairs of the Church. We therefore present unto you our earnest desires of you all. To shew wherein or how many ways you may be useful would easily be done by us and found by you, were you present with us. In all likelihood you will find opportunity enough to draw forth all that healthfulness that God shall afford by you. And we doubt not these advantages will be such, as will fully answer all inconveniences yourselves, churches or plantations may sustain, in this your voyage and short absence from them. Only the sooner you come the better.

[Signed] Warwick,
W. Say and Seale, Ph. Wharton,
Mandeville,
Robert Brooke,

| | |
|---|---|
| Nath. Fiennes, | Wm. Stricland, |
| Gilbert Gerrard, | Henry Darley, |
| Tho. Barrington, | Valentine Walton, |
| Richard Browne, | Will'm Cowleys, |
| Henry Martin, | John Gurdon, |
| Oliver Cromwell, | John Blackiston, |
| A. Haselrig, | Godfrey Rosseville, |
| Tho. Hoyle, | Cor. Holland, |
| Anth. Stapley, | Humphrey Salway, |
| William Hay, | J. Wastill, |
| Wm. Masham, | H. Ruthin, |
| Gilbert Pickering, | Alex. Bruce, |
| Mart. Lumley, | Ro. Cooke, |
| Ol. St. John, | Nath. Barnardiston |
| Sam. Luke, | Isaac Pennington, |
| Ar. Goodwin, | John Franklyn, |
| Miles Corbett, | William Spurstowe. |

## ( C )

*Catalogue of Ministers descended from Mr. Hooker.*

Rev. John Hooker, Rector of Maseworth, Eng.
" Samuel Hooker, Farmington, Conn., 1664.
" Samuel Shepard, Rowley, Mass.
" Daniel Hooker; resided in Wethersfield, Conn.
" Samuel Pierpont, Lyme, Conn., 1724.
" Nathaniel Hooker, West Hartford, Conn.
" John Hooker, Northampton, Mass., 1753.
" Cyprian Strong, Chatham, Conn., 1765.
" Jonathan Edwards, D. D., New Haven, Conn., 1769; Colebrook, Conn., 1795; President of Union College, Schenectady, New York, 1799.
" Timothy Dwight, D. D., LL. D., Greenfield, Conn.; President of Yale College, Conn., 1795.
" Seth Hart, Rector Waterbury and Wallingford, Conn.; Hempstead, Long Island, N. Y.
" William Hart, Rector, Richmond, Va., and Walden, N. Y.

Rev. Giles H. Cowles, D. D., Bristol, Conn., and Austinburgh, Ohio.

" Asahel Hooker, Goshen, Conn., 1795; Norwich, Conn., 1812.

" Asahel Strong, Clinton, N. Y., 1795.

" Solomon Williams, Enosburg, and Addison, Vt.; Potsdam, N. Y.

" Sereno E. Dwight, D. D., Park Street, Boston, 1818; President Hamilton College, N. Y.

" John Pierpont, Hollis Street, Boston, Mass.; Troy, N. Y.

" Timothy Woodbridge, D. D., Greenriver, and Spencertown, N. Y.

" William T. Dwight, D. D., Portland, Me.

" Edward W. Hooker, Greens Farms, Conn., 1821; Bennington, Vt., 1832; Prof. Sac. Rhet. Theol. Inst., Conn., 1844.

" Horace Hooker, Watertown, Conn., 1822; Editor Conn. Observer, 1824; Sec. Conn. Missionary Society.

" Thomas H. Gallaudet, Prin. Conn. Asylum for Deaf and Dumb; Chaplain Conn. Retreat for Insane.

" Jonathan E. Woodbridge, Ware, Mass.; Editor New England Puritan.

' Theodore D. Woolsey, D. D., Prof. Greek

Literature Yale Coll. 1831; Pres. Yale Coll. 1846.

Rev. John A. Yates, D. D., Prof. Orient. Lit. in Union Coll., Schenectady, N. Y.

" Henry B. Hooker, Lanesboro', Mass., 1826; Falmouth, Mass., 1837.

" Robert Ogden Dwight, Missionary A. B. C. F. M., Madura, India.

Mr. Samuel H. Cowles, Licentiate, Andover Seminary, deceased 1824.

Rev. Jeremiah Porter, Western Missionary.

" Richard Hooker, Macon, Ga.

" Tryon Edwards, D. D., Rochester, N. Y.; New London, Conn.

" John E. Edwards, Stonington, Conn.

" Caleb Strong, Montreal, L. Canada.

" Edward S. Dwight, Saco, Me.

" Herman Hooker, Philadelphia, Penn.

*Names of Ministers of the Gospel who married female descendants of Rev. Thomas Hooker.*

Rev. Thomas Shepard, Cambridge, Mass.

" Roger Newton, Milford, Conn.

" John Wilson, Medfield, Mass.

" Grindall Rawson, Mendon, Mass.

" Thomas Weld, Dunstable, Mass.

Rev. James Pierpont, New Haven, Conn.
" Stephen Buckingham, Norwalk, Conn.
" William Russell, Middletown, Conn.
" Isaac Stiles, North Haven, Conn.
" Aaron Burr, Newark, N. J.; Pres. Nassau Hall College, Princeton, N. J.
" Jonathan Edwards, Northampton, Mass.; Stockbridge, Mass.; Pres. Nassau Hall College, Princeton, N. J.
" Benjamin Lord, D. D., Norwich, Conn.
" Solomon Williams, Northampton, Mass.
" Amos Fowler, Guilford, Conn.
" Allen Olcott, Farmington, Conn.
" Amos Bassett, Hebron, Conn.
" James Richards, D. D., Morristown, N. J.; Newark, N. J.; Prof. Chn. Theol., Auburn, N. Y.
" Calvin Chapin, D. D., Rocky-hill, Conn.
" John Eastman, Norwich, and Hanover, N. Y.
" Jonathan Leavitt, Walpole, N. H.
" Claudius Herrick, Woodbridge, Conn.; Teacher, New Haven, Conn.
" Andrew Yates, D. D., East Hartford, Conn.; Prof. Logic and Mor. Phil., Un. Coll., Schenectady, N. Y.
" Alexander Phœnix, Chickopee, Mass.

Rev. Joshua L. Williams, Middletown, Conn.
" Elias Cornelius, D. D., Salem, Mass.; Sec. Amer. Ed. Soc.; Sec. Amer. Board Com. For. Missions.
" Joseph D. Wickham, New Rochelle, N. Y.; Principal of Burr Seminary, Manchester, Vt.
" Amzi Francis, L. Island, N. Y.
" Joshua Leavitt, Stratford, Conn.; Ed. Seaman's Magazine; Sec. Seaman's Fr. Soc.; Ed. N. York Evangelist; Ed. Emancipator, N. York and Boston.
" Solomon Peck, Prof. Lang., Amherst Coll., Mass.; Prof. Latin Lang., Brown Univ., Providence, R. I.; For. Sec. Amer. Baptist Missionary Union.
" Edwards A. Park, D. D., Braintree, Mass.; Prof. Mor. Phil. and Metaph., Amherst Coll., Mass.; Bartlett Prof. Sac. Rhet., Andover Theol. Sem.; Abbott Prof. Chn. Theol., Andover Theol. Sem.
" Samuel Hopkins, Montpelier, Vt.; Saco, Me.
" Josiah F. Goodhue, Shoreham, Vt.
" John N. Lewis, Bristol, N. Y.
" John B. Shaw, Fairhaven, Vt.
" William S. Tyler, Prof. Gr. and Heb. Languages, Amherst Coll., Mass.

Rev. R. H. Seeley, Bristol, Conn.; Springfield, Mass.
" Augustus C. Thompson, Roxbury, Mass.
" E. Janes Montague, Summit, Wisconsin.
" Leonard Bacon, D. D., New Haven, Conn.
" Henry L. Van Meter, Missionary of Amer. Bap. Miss. Union; Arracan.

---

( D )

*Descendants of Mr. Hooker who have served the interests of education, as Professors in institutions for education in the liberal professions, in general literature, intelligence, and the fine arts.*

Hon. John H. Ashmun, Royall Prof. Law, Harvard Univ., Cambridge, Mass.
Charles Hooker, M. D., Prof. Anat. and Phys., Yale Coll., New Haven, Conn.
Mr. Seth Norton, Prof. Lang., Hamilton Coll., N. York.
Edward Hooker, Esq., Teacher, Farmington, Conn.
Mr. Henry E. Dwight, Asso. Prin. New Haven Gymnasium.

Hon. Theodore Dwight, Editor, Hartford, Conn., and New York.

Hon. Daniel Wadsworth, Hartford, Conn.

James G. Percival, M. D., Author and Poet.

Theodore Dwight, Jr., Esq., Editor, Brooklyn, N. Y.

---

(E)

*Descendants of Rev. Thomas Hooker who have occupied important public offices, civil, military, and others.*

Hon. Samuel Hooker, first Mayor of New York City.

" John Hooker, Judge of Sup. Court, Conn.

General Selah Hart, of American army in the war of the Revolution.

Major Roger Hooker, Sec. to Gen. Hart; and in important services of special responsibility, in the Revolutionary war.

Colonel Noadiah Hooker, of Army of the Revolution.

Hon. Timothy Edwards, Stockbridge, Mass., Army Commissioner, in the war of the Revolution.

" Aaron Burr, Vice President U. S. America.

Hon. Pierpont Edwards, District Judge of U. S. Court for Connecticut.

" John Hooker, Springfield, Mass., Judge of Court of Common Pleas.

" Jonathan W. Edwards, Hartford, Conn.

" Henry W. Edwards, Governor of Connecticut.

" Ogden Edwards, Judge of Court in State of New York.

" Lewis Strong, Northampton, Mass., State Senator.

" Thomas Devereux, State's Attorney, North Carolina.

" Henry B. Cowles, M. C., New York.

" Asahel H. Lewis, State Senator, Ohio.

" George Ashmun, State Senator and officer in the Legislature of Massachusetts; also M. C. from Massachusetts.

John Worthington Hooker, Esq., U. S. Indian Agent at Tellicothe, Tennessee.

It is deemed proper to add to the foregoing catalogue, the names of several other men in like stations of public importance and usefulness, some of them in spheres of literary influence and of benevolent effort; and who formed relations by marriage with female descendants of Mr. Hooker.

Hon. Daniel Edwards, Judge Sup. Court, Connecticut.

Col. Jeremiah Wadsworth, of the Army of Revolution.

Hon. Tapping Reeve, Judge Sup. Court, Connecticut.

" Caleb Strong, Governor of Massachusetts.

" Nathaniel Terry, M. C., Connecticut.

William Woolsey, first Treas. Amer. Bible Society, New York.

Hon. Eli P. Ashmun, Senator in Congress, Massachusetts.

" Samuel W. Johnson, Judge Sup. Court, Connecticut.

Eli Whitney, Esq., New Haven, Conn. ;—well known as a national benefactor, by useful inventions.

Hon. William Bristol, Judge U. S. Dist. Court for Connecticut.

Professor Ethan Allen Andrews, Author of valuable text books in Learned Languages.

Frederick A. Packard, Esq., Editor of Publications of Amer. S. S. Union.

Also, to the foregoing catalogues should be added the names of some of Mr. Hooker's descendants who were prominent in the early legislation of the States of Connecticut and Massachusetts.

John Shepard, Esq., Lynn, Mass.
Samuel Newton, Esq., Conn., for 15 legislative sessions.
Thomas Hooker, Esq., Conn., 5 sessions.
Hon. Roger Newton, in Legislature 38 years; Speaker of House Rep. 10 sessions, Conn.
Nathaniel Hooker, Esq., for 6 sessions, Conn.
Joseph Hooker, Esq., Representative and Legislative officer, Conn.
Nathaniel Hooker, Esq., Conn., 6 sessions.
Nathaniel Hooker, Jr., Esq.
Joseph Pierpont, Esq., Conn.
Samuel Hart, Esq., Conn.
Daniel Pierpont, Esq., Conn.
James Hooker, Esq., Conn., for 19 sessions.
John Hooker, Esq., of Farmington, Conn., Representative 23 years; in Upper House 21 sessions; Clerk 2 years, and Speaker 6 years.
John Hooker, Esq., of Berlin, Conn., 7 sessions.
Romanta Norton, Sheriff of Hartford County, Conn.

(F)

Of the descendants of Mr. Hooker, the following, additional to those already mentioned as in public life, entered the profession of Law.

Alfred Cowles, Esq., Illinois.
Theodore Strong, Esq., Northampton, Mass.
John Hooker, Esq., Springfield, Mass.
Josiah Hooker, Esq., Springfield, Mass.
Edward Hooker, Esq., Ohio City, O.
John Hooker, Esq., Columbia, S. C.
John Hooker, Esq., Farmington, Conn.
Charles Olcott, Esq., Medina, O.
Aaron B. Reeve, Esq., Troy, N. Y.
Jonathan E. Porter, Esq., New Haven, Conn.
Jonathan Edwards, Esq., Troy, N. Y.
Walter Edwards, Esq., New York City.
John Starkes Edwards, Esq., New York.
James Hooker, Esq., Poughkeepsie, N. Y.

The following, additional to those mentioned as in Professorships of Medicine, have been Physicians.

Thomas Hooker, M. D., Hartford, Conn.
John R. Lee, M. D., Worcester, Mass.

Thomas G. Lee, M. D., Charlestown, Mass.
Theodore H. Wadsworth, M. D., Austinburgh, O.
John B. Taylor, M. D., Cambridge.
George Hooker, M. D., Longmeadow, Mass.
Worthington Hooker, M. D., Norwich, Conn.
William Hooker, M. D., Westhampton, Mass.
Anson Hooker, M. D., East Cambridge, Mass.
William Hooker, M. D., Dover, N. Y.
Sylvester Wells, M. D., Kensington, Conn.
William Hooker, M. D., Westchester, N. Y.
William Porter, M. D., Hadley, Mass.
Nathaniel Hooker, M. D., Hartford, Conn.
Edward P. Terry, M. D., Hartford, Conn.
Adrian R. Terry, M. D., Detroit, Mich.
Charles A. Terry, M. D., Cleaveland, O.

---

The following additional names of professional men have been received, since the foregoing catalogues were in type.

*Ministers, descendants of Rev. Thomas Hooker.*

Rev. William Russell, Windsor, Conn.
" Noadiah Russell, Thompson, Conn.
" Joseph Welch, resided Troy, N. Y.
" Maurice W. Dwight, Brooklyn, N. Y.
" Nathaniel Dwight, Westchester, Conn.
" Theodore M. Dwight, ———, Georgia.

*Connected by marriage.*

Rev. Moses C. Welch, ———, Conn.

Hon. Matthew T. Russell, Middletown, Conn.
" Cyrus P. Smith, Mayor of Brooklyn, N. Y., (by marriage.)
William H. Russell, Esq., Instructor, New Haven, Conn.

## GENERAL NOTE.

The author has endeavored to make the preceding catalogues as full and accurate as possible. It will probably be found imperfect, still. Any additions and corrections, requisite to its completeness, and which may be furnished, previous to the issue of another edition of this volume, will be carefully made. Information relative to any of the descendants of Rev. Thomas Hooker or their families, is respectfully solicited, by the author.

THE END.

www.ingramcontent.com/pod-product-compliance
Lightning Source LLC
LaVergne TN
LVHW020221110826
845151LV00003B/788

* 9 7 8 1 4 2 5 5 3 2 1 9 2 *